Decision Cases for Advanced Social Work Practice

Thinking Like a Social Worker

Edited by

TERRY A. WOLFER
University of South Carolina

T. LAINE SCALES
Baylor University

THOMSON

BROOKS/COLE

Australia • Canada • Mexico • Singapore • Spain
United Kingdom • United States

THOMSON

BROOKS/COLE

To Regina Yutzy-Wolfer and Glenn Blalock for their constant encouragement, support, and love.

Publisher/Executive Editor: *Lisa Gebo*
Assistant Editor: *Shelley Gesicki*
Editorial Assistant: *Sheila Walsh*
Technology Project Manager: *Barry Connolly*
Marketing Manager: *Caroline Concilla*
Marketing Assistant: *Rebecca Weisman*
Advertising Project Manager: *Tami Strang*
Project Manager, Editorial Production: *Megan E. Hansen*

Art Director: *Vernon Boes*
Print Buyer: *Doreen Suruki*
Permissions Editor: *Kiely Sisk*
Production Service: *Mary E. Deeg, Buuji, Inc.*
Copy Editor: *Cheryl Hauser*
Cover Designer: *Andy Norris*
Compositor: *International Typesetting and Composition*
Printer: *Malloy Incorporated*

Printed in the United States of America
1 2 3 4 5 6 7 09 08 07 06 05

For more information about our products, contact us at:
Thomson Learning Academic Resource Center
1-800-423-0563

For permission to use material from this text or product, submit a request online at
http://www.thomsonrights.com.
Any additional questions about permissions can be submitted by email to
thomsonrights@thomson.com.

Library of Congress Control Number:
2004114373

ISBN 0-534-52196-7

Thomson Higher Education
10 Davis Drive
Belmont, CA 94002-3098
USA

Asia (including India)
Thomson Learning
5 Shenton Way
#01-01 UIC Building
Singapore 068808

Australia/New Zealand
Thomson Learning Australia
102 Dodds Street
Southbank, Victoria 3006
Australia

Canada
Thomson Nelson
1120 Birchmount Road
Toronto, Ontario M1K 5G4
Canada

UK/Europe/Middle East/Africa
Thomson Learning
High Holborn House
50/51 Bedford Row
London WC1R 4LR
United Kingdom

Latin America
Thomson Learning
Seneca, 53
Colonia Polanco
11560 Mexico
D.F. Mexico

Spain (including Portugal)
Thomson Paraninfo
Calle Magallanes, 25
28015 Madrid, Spain

Contents

Preface

As social work educators, we face the challenge of bridging the perennial gap between theory and practice in our classrooms. When we talk with students and practitioners, we see how traditional methods of classroom instruction may not adequately prepare students for the complexities, messiness, and ambiguities of actual social work practice. In the past 5 years we have been interested in finding ways to bring real social work experiences into the classroom setting as instructional tools. Since we discovered case method discussion and the impact it can have on a social worker's development, we have worked on several case collections for classroom use.

The idea for this particular book grew out of Terry's involvement with a case-based capstone course for MSW students at the University of South Carolina College of Social Work. Michael F. Welsh, Associate Professor in the University of South Carolina College of Education, introduced Terry to the decision case method in a course on college teaching. Though inspired by his experience in Michael's course, Terry never imagined where it would lead.

Soon thereafter, during a faculty discussion about ways to strengthen the MSW curriculum, Terry suggested that the faculty develop a case-based course. Rita Rhodes led a small faculty committee to design a new capstone course for MSW students in their final semester before graduation. An energetic, passionate, committed, and highly collaborative group of faculty colleagues brought the capstone course to life, weathered the initial turmoil it caused among students, and worked to make the course what it is now. Beginning in 2000, the founding group of instructors included Errol Bolden, Miriam Freeman, Karen Gray, Julie Miller-Cribbs, Rita Rhodes, Duncan Whyte, and Terry. During the next 4 years, other faculty colleagues and doctoral students who taught the capstone course included Geri Adler, Bill Ayers, Tanya Brice, Brent Cagle, David Cecil, Wendy Sellers Campbell, Michelle Carney, Maryah Fram, Shirley Huisman-Jezowski, Miriam Johnson, Johnny Jones, Chuck Kuhn, Jay Palmer, Vicki Runnion, Glenda Short, and Julie Sprinkle. Their involvement has helped to continually renew and refine the course.

They were fortunate to have the strong support of the College of Social Work administration. Former dean Frank Raymond III provided initial encouragement and financial support of Terry's training in case method teaching and case writing at the Universities of British Columbia and Western Ontario, respectively. Both Dean Raymond and his successor, Dean Leon Ginsberg, provided continuing support for the capstone course and case writing.

Thus far, more than 1,000 MSW students at the University of South Carolina College of Social Work have taken the capstone course before heading off to practice in South Carolina and across the nation. They patiently endured the initial efforts in developing the capstone course and benefited from their instructors' own learning process. Though tales of the course still create anxiety for some students, empirical evaluation and a growing group of graduates, field instructors, and faculty members attest to its value.

Because most of the decision cases in this collection were originally written for the USC capstone course, they come disproportionately from the Southeastern United States. But not all do. About half of the cases took place in other regions of the United States and were reported by doctoral students, field instructors, or faculty members after they moved to South Carolina. Although most of the cases have been disguised to protect individuals and organizations, we avoided making changes (i.e., gender, ethnicity, region) that would alter case dynamics. In the interest of case fidelity, we retained approximate dates and numerous other details that experienced practitioners know make a difference when assessing a situation.

These decision cases come from many fields of practice and involve social workers in diverse practice roles. Because they were originally developed for the USC capstone course, the mix of cases reflects the diverse fields and roles for which USC students prepare. Although most social work students, like those at USC, intend to enter direct practice, we think it is essential for them to understand the social policies and administrative contexts that inevitably and profoundly influence their work. Further, we think it is important for social work students to understand the perspectives of their supervisors and agency administrators, including the effects of interpersonal dynamics at those levels. Conversely, we think it is essential for students planning careers in agency administration, community organizing, policy development, or social work research to understand the realities of social work direct practice because they will supervise, engage, influence, or evaluate their colleagues in those roles. In all these roles, social workers repeatedly encounter novel and surprising situations. We share a vision for social work that strives to hold our profession's differences in tension, and we see these differences as strengths.

In addition to what students may learn about unfamiliar social work settings and interventions, these cases provide opportunity for practicing the fundamental skills of formulating and analyzing problems, and deciding how to respond. The cases depict complex and challenging practice situations. We do not offer the cases as examples of either good or poor practice but rather as puzzles to resolve together.

Many people have assisted us in learning case method teaching and case writing and helped us introduce the method to our colleagues and students. I (Terry) would like to thank Michael Welsh who remains a good friend, mentor, and collaborator on case method teaching, and who also introduced me to the North American Case Research Association. I thank deans Raymond and Ginsberg for their continuing support of the capstone course, faculty development, and case writing. I also thank colleagues Rita Rhodes and Karen Gray for their committed leadership of the capstone faculty group, and Vicki Runnion for collaboration on another case project. In compiling this case collection, I am deeply grateful to Laine Scales, a good friend and colleague, who shared editorial responsibilities for this and a companion case collection for BSW students. From all these people I have learned much.

I (Laine) would like to thank my friend Terry, with whom I have enjoyed collaborating on so many different kinds of professional projects, for initially introducing me to case method teaching 4 years ago and for inviting me into this project. Terry also did me a great favor when he introduced me to the Pace University Center for Case Studies in Education and its yearly conference in Vancouver, British Columbia, Enlivening Teaching: Using Discipline-Based Cases and Classroom Research to Improve Learning and Teaching. There I began to build a foundation in case method teaching and found helpful mentors among the conference leaders, particularly Dr. Rita Silverman and Dr. John Boeher. I also am indebted to my colleagues in the Baylor University School of Social Work for their willingness to embrace case method teaching, to pilot our cases, and to create new cases to stimulate our students.

Together, we have many people to thank, beginning with the case reporters who provided detailed information about actual difficult situations from their professional experience. Without their thorough and self-reflective reporting, this collection would obviously not be possible. We also thank the case authors, many of whom tackled a new style of writing and persisted through multiple revisions to ensure the accuracy and clarity of these accounts. In that regard, we also value the helpful feedback from four anonymous reviewers. We appreciate Lisa Gebo and Caroline Concillia of Brooks/Cole for their initial interest in and support of this new approach to case writing, and Mary Deeg and the team at Buuji who worked steadily and efficiently to prepare the manuscript.

We hope that you will find this casebook a useful resource for class discussions that help you practice "thinking like a social worker." Jump in, the water's fine.

About the Editors

Terry A. Wolfer, PhD, is an associate professor in the College of Social Work at the University of South Carolina (Columbia). He has authored or coauthored 20 articles and several additional manuscripts on social work education, faith-based social services, and psychological trauma. He coedited *Spirituality and Religion in Social Work Practice: Decision Cases with Teaching Notes* (CSWE, 2002). He currently serves as an associate editor for the journal *Social Work and Christianity*. He is a recipient of the Social Work Leadership Development Award from the Project on Death in America for writing a collection of decision cases on death and dying in social work practice. Dr. Wolfer has served on the boards of several social service organizations and the North American Association of Christians in Social Work. He recently completed a sabbatical as a visiting scholar at the University of Queensland (Brisbane, Australia). Before joining the faculty at South Carolina, Dr. Wolfer was a visiting instructor at the University of Illinois at Chicago and a lecturer at the University of Chicago.

T. Laine Scales, PhD, is an associate professor of Social Work at Baylor University in Waco, Texas. She wrote *All That Fits a Woman: Educating Southern Baptist Women for Charity and Mission, 1907–1926* (Mercer University Press, 2000) and has coedited four books including *Spirituality and Religion in Social Work Practice: Decision Cases with Teaching Notes* (CSWE, 2002) and *Rural Social Work: Building Assets to Sustain Communities* (Wadsworth, 2004). She has published over a dozen articles and chapters on various social work topics and currently serves as an associate editor for the journal *Social Work and Christianity*.

Dr. Scales has held leadership positions in National Association of Social Workers, Texas Chapter and North American Association of Christians in Social Work. Prior to joining the faculty of Baylor, Dr. Scales taught at Stephen F. Austin State University in Nacogdoches, Texas, and Palm Beach Atlantic College in West Palm Beach, Florida.

AUTHOR BIOGRAPHIES

Heather Bennett, BS, is a MSW student in the College of Social Work at the University of South Carolina.

Brent E. Cagle, MSW, is a doctoral candidate in the College of Social Work at the University of South Carolina. He holds graduate degrees in English and social work and has worked as a university and community college teacher, a foster care worker, and an in-home therapist with runaway adolescents and their families. His scholarly interests include the study of queer youth organizations and seeking strengths-based approaches to understanding queer youth development, policy formulation, and program building.

Karen A. Gray, PhD, is an assistant professor in the College of Social Work at the University of South Carolina. She has 17 years of social work practice experience and has published in the areas of poverty and macro social work practice. Her current research interests are women and children's lives in and out of poverty and macro social work practice.

Miriam McNown Johnson, PhD, is an associate professor in the College of Social Work at the University of South Carolina. She has more than 20 years of practice experience, mostly with children in out-of-home care and their families, but also with refugee resettlement programs. Her research interests include consumerism and student perceptions of strengths in diverse populations. She is coauthor of *Human Behavior and the Larger Social Environment: A New Synthesis* (Allyn and Bacon, 2005).

Carl D. Maas, LMSW, MPH, is the quality assurance manager for Prevent Child Abuse South Carolina, Healthy Families South Carolina program. Maas teaches in the College of Social Work at the University of South Carolina as an adjunct instructor. He has 11 years experience in community development, child welfare, community mental health, domestic violence, and services for Latino/Hispanic families.

Robert Jay Palmer, MSW, is a doctoral candidate and adjunct instructor in the College of Social Work at the University of South Carolina. A practicing social worker for 7 years, he has worked with HIV-positive, homeless, and developmentally disabled populations. He is currently a board member of the Society for Spirituality and Social Work and a former board member of the Nebraska Chapter of NASW.

Melissa C. Reitmeier, LMSW, is a doctoral candidate in the College of Social Work at the University of South Carolina. She is also the director of quality assurance with the state's protection and advocacy system for people with disabilities, as well as a contract therapist with South Carolina Center for Dialectical Behavior Therapy. She has taught several social work courses in both graduate and undergraduate programs at the University of South Carolina and Limestone College. Her research interests include social work education, welfare reform, and rural poverty.

Vicki M. Runnion, MSSW, is a social work coordinator at Hospice & Palliative Care of Southern Indiana. She has been involved in hospice work, in various roles, since 1979. She is a recipient of the Social Work Leadership Development Award from the Project on Death in America, and is particularly interested in end-of-life and loss issues for people with intellectual disabilities. She has taught social work as an adjunct instructor at the University of Louisville, University of South Carolina, and Columbia College (SC).

F. Matthew Schobert, Jr., M.Div., LMSW, is unit manager of a structured-care home unit for adolescent boys at Methodist Children's Home in Waco, Texas. He provides intensive case management and clinical social services to youth and their families. He also lectures in the Baylor Interdisciplinary Core Program at Baylor University in Waco, Texas, and serves as a board member of an international nonprofit. He publishes and presents in the fields of social work and theology.

Julie E. Sprinkle, LMSW, is a doctoral candidate and adjunct professor in the College of Social Work at the University of South Carolina. She has several years of experience in program evaluation, health, and mental health. Her research interests include gender wage inequality, intimate partner violence, and child and adolescent violence prevention.

Terry A. Wolfer, PhD, is an associate professor in the College of Social Work at the University of South Carolina. He teaches micro practice, macro practice, research and evaluation, and a capstone course. Previously, he practiced in the fields of child welfare and family services. His scholarly interests include social work education, outcome evaluation, psychological trauma, volunteerism, and faith-based social services.

Jeanette Ucci, MSW, is the social services director at Beaufont Health Care Center, a rehabilitation and long-term care facility in Richmond, Virginia, and a graduate of the College of Social Work at the University of South Carolina.

PART I

To the Student

Chapter 1

An Introduction to Decision Cases and Case Method Learning

TERRY A. WOLFER

"Good judgment comes from experience.
Experience comes from bad judgment."

WALTER WRISTON
(CITED IN BRUNER, 1999, p. xxiii)

The case method of learning typically involves in-depth class discussions based on detailed, open-ended accounts of actual practice situations. These accounts, referred to as decision cases, require students to formulate the problems and decide on potential courses of action. The case analyses and class discussions help students learn to apply theory to practice and to develop important problem-solving and critical-thinking skills. Because this particular form of cases may be unfamiliar to you, we intend this introductory chapter to provide background information on cases and the case method. This chapter will do the following:

1. Consider the ubiquitous nature of cases and decision making in professional social work education and practice.

2. Differentiate cases for decision making from the more common cases for examples or illustration.

3. Help students understand how case discussions differ, both philosophically and practically, from traditional approaches to social work education.

4. Identify general learning outcomes associated with analyzing and discussing decision cases, and the importance of these outcomes for social work practice.

5. Explain where these cases came from, and how they were written.

In the next chapter, we provide concrete tips for analyzing and preparing to discuss cases.

WHAT IS YOUR EXPERIENCE WITH CASES?

No doubt, you are well acquainted with the use of cases in your social work program. Many social work instructors and textbook authors provide cases to aid your understanding of social work practice. In field supervision, you likely discuss individual cases and the problems or challenges these pose for you. In your field practicum or social work employment, you may measure your workload in terms of the number of cases you carry at any point in time.

This collection of cases is similar in some ways to these various types of cases but different in other important ways. Like cases in your classrooms or textbooks, these cases were developed for teaching purposes. However, these cases have a more specific teaching purpose that probably differs from published cases with which you may be familiar. In social work education, most published cases have an illustrative purpose. They provide examples of good practice, or even exemplars for you to emulate. Such cases depict difficult practice situations and show how social workers dealt with these situations. They typically show how a social work theory was applied in the particular situation, providing insight or understanding, or how a social work intervention was carried out, providing guidance in use of the intervention. In short, such cases show you how some theory or intervention applies to practice or, more simply, how the theory or intervention *works*.

Discussing cases with your social work field instructor or supervisor also has a teaching purpose, though it might be more accurate to refer to this as a learning purpose. In supervision, your field instructor "looks over your shoulder" to ensure that things are going well and to provide direction as necessary. When you discuss difficult cases with your field instructor, you may review what has happened, what you have tried to do, and so on. Initially, your supervisor carries important responsibility for guiding your efforts. But as you gain practice experience, you will increasingly use supervision to make collaborative decisions about what to do next. In these situations, your field instructor or supervisor is not directing your work so much as helping you decide how to proceed, what to try, what the likely consequences will be, and so on. This type of supervision shifts the focus from the past to the present and future, from what happened to what to do next. And it shifts the emphasis from your instructor "teaching you what to do" to the two of you (or the supervision group) collaboratively figuring out what to do. This approach to supervision is common in professional social work practice, and this set of decision cases is intended to resemble and promote it.

In direct practice settings especially, the set of cases (caseload) for which you have responsibility also provides a shorthand way of referring to your workload. In this usage, a case refers to the client system for which you have some professional responsibility. The client may be understood to be an individual, a couple, or a family unit.

In this casebook, however, the word *case* does not refer to cases of this type. Instead, we use *case* for referring to specific situations in professional practice that pose problems and dilemmas, and these situations are more like those described in the previous paragraph. Furthermore, these cases may come from any level of social work practice. As a result, the client system may include a supervisee, program, organization, community, or state in addition to individuals, families, or groups in direct practice. This brief reflection reveals how ubiquitous cases are in professional social work practice, and also alerts us to some important distinctions in use of the term.

CASES IN SOCIAL WORK EDUCATION

The use of cases is nothing new. For more than 100 years, social work instructors have used cases in the classroom to educate students (Fisher, 1978; Reitmeier, 2002; e.g., Reynolds, 1942; Towle, 1954). Over time, these cases have taken many forms, ranging from brief vignettes only a few sentences or paragraphs long to complex book-length accounts.

Merseth (1996) identified three basic educational purposes for using cases: cases as examples or exemplars to illustrate practice, cases as foci for reflecting on practice, or cases as opportunities to practice decision making. For the first purpose, mentioned above, cases provide concrete and specific examples of how professional theories or interventions apply in practice situations. As illustrations, cases can help students understand theoretical content and practice skills. During the past few decades, most of the available social work casebooks provide cases for this purpose (e.g., Amodeo, Schofield, Duffy, Jones, Zimmerman, & Delgado, 1997; Haulotte & Kretzschmar, 2001; LeCroy, 1999; McClelland, Austin, & Este, 1998; Rivas & Hull, 2000).

Although most cases in social work education have an illustrative purpose, the cases here have primarily a decision-making purpose. They resemble the type of cases that social workers take to their supervisors when they are uncertain how to understand a situation or how to respond. In fact, the cases in this collection troubled the practitioners who experienced and reported them. For some, the situations remain perplexing months (and even years) after they occurred.

Rather than provide good examples of how practice theories or interventions might work, these cases present challenging problem-solving opportunities. As a result, they provide opportunities for you to practice decision making, to refine the skills you need in social work practice. Like social work practice dilemmas you might take to a supervisor, these cases present messy, ambiguous, problematic situations that invite and merit professional thinking and intervention. Discussing these challenging cases will clarify the funda-mental importance of problem framing or formulation; they require you to bring structure to complex, ill-structured situations. Having formulated the problems, you must decide what to do about the various situations. As you will see, many social work interventions may be possible or even relevant in partic-ular cases but these interventions will vary by the extent to which they actu-ally help resolve the basic dilemmas. Class discussions will clarify the probable consequences of various formulations and strategies, and help you refine your decision-making processes.

DISTINGUISHING DECISION CASES
FROM OTHER TYPES

In defining decision cases, scholars note several characteristics that distinguish them from other types of cases. For example, Mauffette-Leenders, Erskine, and Leenders (1997) define a decision case as "a description of an actual situation, commonly involving a decision, a challenge, an opportunity, a problem or issue faced by a person (or persons) in an organization. The case allows [the reader] to step figuratively into the position of the particular decision maker" (p. 2). Similarly, Christensen and Hansen (1987) define a decision case as:

> a partial, historical, clinical study of a situation which has confronted a . . .
> [practitioner]. Presented in narrative form to encourage student
> involvement, it provides data—substantive and process—essential to an
> analysis of a specific situation, for the framing of alternative action
> programs, and for their implementation recognizing the complexity and
> ambiguity of the practical world. (p. 27)

These definitions highlight several key characteristics of decision cases.

Like case examples or exemplars, decision cases provide accounts of social work practice situations but they differ in several important ways (Wolfer, 2003). Perhaps most distinctively, decision cases involve a dilemma of some sort for the practitioner and the written cases end with the situation unre-solved (Leenders, Mauffette-Leenders, & Erskine, 2001; Lynn, 1999; Weaver, Kowalski, & Pfaller, 1994). As a result, students must "untangle situations that are complex and undefined and impose a coherence of their own making" (Barnes, 1989, p. 17; cited in Merseth, 1996, p. 729). By presenting incomplete and ill-structured or "messy" situations (Boehrer & Linsky, 1990), decision cases especially stimulate readers to analyze the information they contain and formulate problems, and then to decide how to intervene in the situations. In short, open-ended cases spur readers to seek resolution.

Furthermore, decision cases generally depict actual situations encountered by social work practitioners rather than generic or composite situations. While some identifying information may be disguised to protect individuals and organizations, case writers try to avoid making any changes to cases that alter case dynamics (Cossom, 1991). Indeed, case writers construct decision cases based on multiple interviews with key participants, usually the protagonist and sometimes other people (Leenders et al., 2001; Lynn, 1999; Naumes & Naumes, 1999; Welsh, 1999). Case writers gather detailed information, including conversational dialogue as case reporters remember it (Weaver et al., 1994). As a result, cases reflect the perspectives of case reporters, with both the strengths and limitations of their subjectivity. Well-written cases "put the student reader squarely in the shoes of the social worker" (Cossom, 1991, p. 141). They allow readers to "inhabit" or empathize with the world of the case reporter, to both know and "feel" the information that constitutes the problematic situation.

Decision cases typically differ from example cases in several additional ways. They often include more background information than example cases, including details about the time period, the social service agency and other organizations involved, organizational and social policies, and the community setting. In this way, cases better reflect the "complex, messy, context-specific activity" of professional practice (Merseth, 1996, p. 728). As experienced practitioners recognize, such information often plays an essential role in situations and their possible resolution (Doyle, 1990; Shulman, 1992). However, some of the included case details may be extraneous and potentially distracting, requiring readers to sort through the data, just as they must do in actual practice (Weaver et al., 1994).

Typically, decision cases also include more information about the protagonists than example cases, because this information also plays an essential part in the situations (Weaver et al., 1994; Wolfer, 2003). Where example cases often invite readers to identify with a generic social worker (i.e., "Ms. Green"), decision cases provide details about the social worker that may be relevant for case dynamics. Putting this information on the page helps readers to recognize and consider how the self of the social worker may interact with problems and their resolution. Further, it encourages readers to reflect on how their own selves may also have consequences in professional practice.

Usually, decision cases do not include much theoretical content, except when case reporters explicitly mention it themselves. In professional practice, most situations do not present with explicit theoretical frameworks (Lynn, 1999; Sykes & Bird, 1992). Decision cases simply reflect that lack of explicit theory. As a result, the raw case data requires that readers supply theory for understanding the situations and helps them come to understand the critical need to do so (i.e., theory provides a "handle" on case situations). It also allows instructors considerable latitude in discussing cases from different theoretical perspectives.

These cases may provide little new information about topics you have been learning in other courses (though you may learn about particular social work settings, interventions, or problems with which you are unfamiliar). Instead, they emphasize the use of previous learning, especially in novel situations. In that way, these cases resemble social work practice, and discussing these cases resembles peer supervision. The cases themselves seldom make clear what theory or interventions might be suitable. You must decide about that, drawing from what you have learned up to this point. Hopefully, by providing opportunities for you to practice decision making in complex and challenging situations, analyzing and discussing the cases will also help you to refine your decision-making skills and to become a more self-reflective decision maker. Some of the things you will learn from discussing these cases would likely have occurred during your initial years of social work employment. But by discussing these cases, you can accelerate your learning and aid your successful transition to professional social work practice.

For these reasons, this collection of decision cases is especially well suited for use in capstone courses or integrative field seminars. For all students, these cases help provide a bridge between theory and practice, between the classroom and their agency settings. For students nearing completion of their educational programs, these cases may assist their transition from student to practitioner as they assume greater decision-making responsibility.

OUTCOMES OF DECISION CASE LEARNING

In part, the differences between novices and experienced practitioners may have less to do with what they know than with how they use their knowledge (Livingston & Borko, 1989). Business educators Barnes, Christensen, and Hansen (1994) argue that case method instruction helps to develop in students an applied "administrative point of view" (p. 50). In other words, case method instruction helps business students to develop the perspective of experienced business administrators or practitioners. In social work, we could refer to this as "thinking like a social worker" (hence the title of this book).

Barnes, Christensen, and Hansen suggest that an administrative point of view includes several components. These are (1) a focus on understanding the specific context; (2) a sense for appropriate boundaries; (3) sensitivity to interrelationships; (4) examining and understanding any situation from a multidimensional point of view; (5) accepting personal responsibility for the solution of organizational problem; and (6) an action orientation (pp. 50–51). These components reflect a thoroughly systemic approach to understanding practice.

Furthermore, the latter component (6) above, an action orientation, includes several dimensions acquired through practice experience. These dimensions are (a) a sense of the possible; (b) willingness to make decisions on the basis of imperfect and limited data; (c) a sense of the critical aspects of a situation; (d) the ability to combine discipline and creativity; (e) skill in converting targets into accomplishments; and (f) an appreciation of the major limitations of professional action (Barnes et al., p. 51). Together, they distinguish expert practitioners from novices. In short, the concept of an administrative or practitioner point of view redirects our attention from what students know to their ability to use their knowledge judiciously. From this perspective, theoretical knowledge and technical skill are essential but insufficient for competent practice. Not only must competent professionals have knowledge and skills, they must know how to use them, and exercise good judgment in doing so.

Although the knowledge, skill, and value bases differ significantly between business and social work, we think there are some important parallels between how business and social work professionals need to think and act in professional practice. As Barnes and his colleagues argue, competent practice requires profoundly systemic ways of thinking and deciding. Hopefully, analyzing and discussing these cases will help you to acquire some of the attitudes, knowledge, and skills that experienced social workers identify as critical to their professional success.

Several teacher educators identify other outcomes of case method learning. At the most basic level, cases convey information or declarative knowledge, that is, *what* to know. For example, education researchers have explored the effectiveness of cases for introducing multicultural perspectives, pedagogical theory, and mathematics content (e.g., Merseth, 1996). At a deeper level, cases can promote different ways of thinking or procedural knowledge, that is, *how* to know and do. For example, education researchers have begun to explore the effectiveness of cases for developing problem-solving and decision-making skills, beliefs about professional authority and personal efficacy, more realistic perspectives on the complexities of practice (and new ways of looking at practice), and habits of reflection (Merseth, 1996).

Lundeberg (1999), another teacher educator, provides an alternative conceptual framework for understanding case method learning outcomes. Based on empirical research, she reports benefits in five categories, most of which relate to different ways of thinking. The first category, theoretical and practical understandings, combines two kinds of knowledge that researchers have often separated. She combines them because of the ways instructors can use cases for generating theory from practice, encouraging students to apply theory in practical situations, and for helping students discover when and how theories may be useful (p. 4). The second category, improved reasoning and reflective decision making, reflects a basic purpose of case method instruction. Decision cases are specifically designed for helping students develop their abilities: "to identify, frame, or find a problem; consider problems from multiple perspectives; provide solutions for problems identified; and consider the consequences and ethical ramifications of these solutions" (p. 8). As another teacher educator notes, "Many students see problems as no more

than common-sense, obvious difficulties. They have not developed the idea
that problems are constructed and can be constructed in more and less fruit-
ful ways" (Kleinfield, 1991, p. 7; cited in Lundeberg, 1999, p. 9). Case discussions provide significant opportunities for developing more sophisticated
decision-making abilities. The growth of reasoning relates to a third category,
metacognition, the process of reflecting on one's own thinking processes
(Lundeberg, 1999, p. 12). While awareness of thinking and learning processes
is obviously important for classroom teachers, it has an important parallel for
social workers. Thinking and learning processes are part of a broader category
of change processes. Case discussions may help students better understand the
nature and difficulty of change processes, especially as they become more
self-reflective regarding their own learning. For education students, metacog-
nitions are closely related to a fourth category, beliefs about learning (p. 14).
Early literature on cognitive change suggested that awareness of one's own
beliefs and how they conflict with empirically based ideas about learning
would lead to change in beliefs. More recent literature reveals that cognitive
change is less rational and more dependent on social interaction. Applying
this insight to change processes more generally, case method may provide
experience and insight regarding the importance of relationship dynamics in
social work interventions, whether at the micro or macro level. Lundeberg
refers to a final category of benefits as social, ethical, and epistemological
growth (p. 15). Her colleague, Harrington (1994), wrote:

> The knowledge of most worth is brought into being dialogically. It is said
> and heard in multiple ways—transformed in the sharing—enriched
> through multiplicity. Dialogue allows students to become aware of what
> they share in common, as well as the uniqueness of each of them as
> individuals. (p. 192; cited in Lundeberg, 1999, p. 16)

Deep appreciation for dialogue, as a means of comprehending similarity and
difference, represents a profound type of growth fostered by case method.
Dialogue is relevant for social work practice with clients but also for interaction with colleagues, agencies, and communities. And it leads to greater appreciation for the ethical context of practice. In their book, Lundeberg and her
colleagues review the empirical evidence for these benefits of case method
learning (Lundeberg, Levin, & Harrington, 1999).

   Although originally identified in the context of teacher education, these
benefits of case method learning seem highly relevant for social work practice
as well. Competent practice requires both theoretical and practical knowledge,
reasoning and reflective decision-making skills, metacognitive awareness
(especially regarding change processes), appropriate beliefs about change, and
social, ethical, and epistemological growth. Unfortunately, these significant
benefits of case method learning are sometimes overlooked in social work
education, or at least not addressed in formal ways. In that respect, case
method may prove to be a valuable supplement to the traditional classroom.

CASE METHOD TEACHING

To most fully exploit the teaching potential of decision cases, instructors must use a "case method teaching" approach (Barnes et al., 1994; Cossom, 1991; Erskine, Leenders, & Mauffette-Leenders, 1998; Lundeberg et al., 1999; Lynn, 1999; Welty, 1989). Because this approach may differ from what your instructors normally do, it may be helpful for you to have some advance warning about what they may do differently and to be aware of their reasons for it. Case method teaching relies heavily on discussion, and case method instructors essentially lead discussions by asking questions (Boehrer & Linsky, 1990). The overarching questions are twofold: What is the problem? And what would you do about it? In classroom discussions, however, instructors may not actually ask these two basic questions. Instead, they ask many more specific questions designed to explore these two questions. Instructors formulate and select questions based partly on their instructional goals, what background knowledge students bring to the discussion, and the direction and flow of the immediate discussion. As discussions develop, instructors may encourage individual students to elaborate on their perspectives, seek divergent viewpoints from other students, and ask about connections or discrepancies between new comments and previous comments. Although it sometimes frustrates students, case method instructors consistently refrain from providing their own perspectives or opinions about the cases. Rather than identify possible errors of fact or judgment themselves, instructors promote critical thinking by asking good questions. Indeed, case method instructors consider students' increasing ability to pose good questions, as importance evidence of their learning (Boehrer & Linsky, 1990).

Much like group therapists, case method instructors must also attend to the level of discussion process (Lundeberg et al., 1999; Welty, 1989). For example, instructors seek to distribute speaking turns, steering the discussion away from overly talkative students toward quieter students. They monitor perceptions of classroom safety, and consider the effects of their own and students' contributions. In their questioning, they sometimes push students to express disagreements and at other times allow students to go more slowly. More than some other teaching approaches, case method teaching requires that instructors listen well (Christensen, 1991; Leonard, 1991), to maintain simultaneous awareness of both discussion content and discussion process.

THE CASES

This book includes a diverse mix of cases, some involving predominantly micro settings and issues and others involving predominantly macro settings and issues. In ways that may surprise you, however, you will come to see how micro and macro issues are frequently intertwined, how the traditional distinction between micro and macro practice does not work well at times in actual practice. These cases make clear the systemic nature of reality and provide support for the widespread emphasis on systems thinking in social work education. We created the mix of cases to reinforce this point.

Occasionally, some students object to the mix of cases. Students who may be focusing on micro practice, for example, may not understand why they should know or care about political intrigue in policy making at the state level. Or students who may be focusing on macro practice may not understand why they should be familiar with controversial practice interventions for individual clients. Hopefully, this collection will help you to see common threads across these situations, to develop your skills of assessment and decision making, and to better understand the interactive nature of systems. Discussing these cases will also help you to return to your own area of specialization with increased insight, flexibility, and creativity. These assertions may prompt you to wonder about the intended benefits of learning with decision cases.

WHERE THESE CASES CAME FROM, AND HOW THEY WERE WRITTEN

Most of the cases in this collection were originally developed for a case-based capstone course at the University of South Carolina's College of Social Work (Wolfer, Freeman, & Rhodes, 2001). Because we intended the cases for students in the final semester of the MSW program, the cases all involve MSW-level practitioners. Most of the cases were reported by doctoral students, faculty members, field instructors, or recent graduates of the college. As a result, the cases come disproportionately from the southeastern United States. But because many people at the college, in each of those categories, have moved to South Carolina from other areas of the United States, the cases come from other parts of the country as well. To qualify for use in the course and inclusion in this case collection, cases must have met several criteria:

1. The situation may be drawn from any field of social work practice.
2. The situation may be drawn from direct practice with individuals, families or groups, or indirect practice with organizations or communities.
3. The situation must include a social worker with some critical decision-making responsibility (the social worker serves as the protagonist).
4. The situation must involve some type of dilemma for the social worker. The dilemma may include, for example, conflicting values or ethical principles held by individual clients, their families, the social worker, the social work organization, or social policies. In the best cases, competent social workers may disagree about appropriate responses to the dilemma.

5. The social worker must have (or be working toward) an MSW degree, so that MSW students can reasonably identify with and learn from his or her dilemma.

6. Finally, the social worker must be interested and willing to report the situation in confidential interviews with a case writer.

As implied by these criteria, the cases were all field researched. That is, they were all based on in-depth interviews with individual social workers who agreed to report their experiences. More specifically, the cases were researched and written using a conjoint, repeated interview process developed by Welsh (1999). It typically consisted of several steps.

First, before the case reporting sessions, case reporters prepared brief written accounts of a problem or decision they actually faced in social work practice. These accounts helped case writers determine the likely appropriateness of a case dilemma before they began in-depth research.

Second, during the reporting sessions, case reporters told case writing teams the story behind their accounts. In addition to the case reporter and case writer, each team typically included one or two additional social workers from the case reporter's field of practice to assist with questioning. Following Welsh (1999), we have found that conjoint interviews broaden and deepen the case writer's understanding of the case situation. We audiotaped these interviews to collect detailed descriptions and numerous direct quotes from case reporters.

Third, after the reporting session, the case writer(s) prepared a working draft of the case that included a title, an opening paragraph or introductory "hook," necessary background sections, and the story line with descriptions and quotes.

Fourth, case writers sought additional information from case reporters as needed, exchanged working drafts with the case reporter, co-interviewers, and editors for editorial feedback, and returned a final draft to the case reporter for confirmation. Case writers did not release cases for publication until case reporters signed release forms indicating they felt satisfied that the written cases accurately reflected their experiences and adequately disguised the situation.

In consultation with the case reporters, we disguised the cases to protect them, their clients, and their social service organizations. In most cases, the disguise involved changing names of people, organizations, and places, and selected details. As much as possible, however, we avoided changing case data that would alter essential case dynamics. For example, we did not change the gender of case reporters or clients, or the geographic regions in which cases occurred. In subtle ways, these and similar factors influence how the case situations developed and how they may be interpreted, and we did not want to undermine the reality of what the case reporters experienced. As suggested above, learning to take account of such details distinguishes expert practitioners from novices.

Whatever you think of particular decision cases in the collection, avoid jumping to conclusions. The case reporters have been generous and courageous in telling about particularly challenging, even troubling situations they have faced in professional practice. For that, we are most grateful. For some case reporters, the situations continue to frustrate, perplex and concern them, and that was part of the reason they agreed to report their cases.

READING THE CASES

The decision cases in this collection can be read on several levels. On one level, they simply depict a variety of settings that employ social workers and the types of situations that occasionally crop up in those settings. Obviously, the cases represent only a small sample of practice fields (e.g., homelessness, mental health, wife abuse, public education, and international community development).

On a second level, the cases depict specific challenges that individual social workers encountered in certain settings and at certain points in time. From a systems perspective, the multiple and overlapping factors will be quite evident, though the specifics vary from case to case. In various combinations, these factors include client needs and values; social worker needs, values and skills; needs and values of other individuals related to the client(s); organizational philosophies, policies and procedures; professional social work values and ethics; and government policies and laws. These multiple factors create the complex and particular environments in which social workers must function, and which they must carefully consider when attempting to resolve the dilemmas.

But on a third, more abstract level, the cases also reflect common challenges of social work practice across settings (and, we might add, of human experience). These include, for example, balancing client and organizational needs, resolving contradictory policy requirements, making decisions with incomplete information, identifying the appropriate limits of professional intervention, anticipating unintended consequences of decisions, and resolving value or ethical dilemmas.

As you read, try to consider the cases on each of these levels. You may begin by asking yourself, "What is this case about?" Repeatedly asking and answering this question can help you reach for deeper levels of understanding. The next chapter goes further in suggesting ways to read and analyze the cases and to prepare for discussing them.

REFERENCES

Amodeo, M., Schofield, R., Duffy, T., Jones, K., Zimmerman, T., & Delgado, M. (Eds.). (1997). *Social work approaches to alcohol and other drug problems: Case studies and teaching tools.* Alexandria, VA: Council on Social Work Education.

Barnes, L. B., Christensen, C. R., & Hansen, A. J. (1994). *Teaching and the case method* (3rd ed.). Boston: Harvard Business School Press.

Boehrer, J., & Linsky, M. (1990). Teaching with cases: Learning to question. In M. D. Svinicki (Ed.), *The changing face of college teaching* (pp. 41–57). San Francisco: Jossey-Bass.

Bruner, R. F. (1999). Note to the student: How to study and discuss cases. In *Case studies in finance: Managing for corporate value creation* (3rd ed.; pp. xxiii–xxvi). Boston: Irwin McGraw-Hill.

[Also available online at http://faculty.
darden.virginia.edu/brunerb/resources_
studentnote.htm]

Christensen, C. R. (1991). The discussion
teacher in action: Questioning, listening,
and response. In C. R. Christensen,
D. A. Garvin, & A. Sweet (Eds.), *Education
for judgment: The artistry of discussion leadership* (pp. 153–172). Boston: Harvard
Business School Press.

Christensen, C. R., & Hansen, A. (1987).
Teaching and the case method. Boston:
Harvard Business School Press.

Cossom, J. (1991). Teaching from cases:
Education for critical thinking. *Journal
of Teaching in Social Work, 5*(1), 139–155.

Doyle, W. (1990). Case methods in the education of teachers. *Teacher Education
Quarterly, 17*(1), 7–16.

Erskine, J. A., Leenders, M. R., & Mauffette-
Leenders, L. A. (1998). *Teaching with cases*
(3rd ed.). London, ONT: Ivey
Publishing, Ivey School of Business
Administration, The University of
Western Ontario.

Fisher, C. F. (1978). Being there vicariously
by case studies. In M. Ohmer and
Associates (Ed.), *On college teaching: A
guide to contemporary practices* (pp. 258–285).
San Francisco: Jossey-Bass.

Harrington, H. (1994). Teaching and knowing. *Journal of Teacher Education, 45*(3),
190–198.

Haulotte, S. M., & Kretzschmar, J. A. (Eds.).
(2001). *Case scenarios for teaching and
learning social work practice.* Alexandria,
VA: Council on Social Work
Education.

LeCroy, C. W. (1999). *Case studies in social
work practice* (2nd ed.). Pacific Grove,
CA: Brooks/Cole.

Leenders, M. R., Mauffette-Leenders, L. A.,
& Erskine, J. A. (2001). *Writing cases* (4th
ed.). London, ONT: Ivey Publishing,
Ivey School of Business Administration,
The University of Western Ontario.

Leonard, H. B. (1991). With open ears:
Listening and the art of discussion lead-
ing. In C. R. Christensen, D. A. Garvin,
& A. Sweet (Eds.), *Education for judgment:
The artistry of discussion leadership*
(pp. 137–151). Boston: Harvard Business
School Press.

Livingston, C., & Borko, H. (1989). Expert-
novice difference in teaching: A cognitive analysis and implications for teacher
education. *Journal of Teacher Education,
40*(4), 36–42.

Lundeberg, M. A. (1999). Discovering teaching and learning through cases. In M. A.
Lundeberg, B. B. Levin, & H. L.
Harrington (Eds.), *Who learns what from
cases and how? The research base for teaching
with cases* (pp. 3–23). Mahwah, NJ:
Lawrence Erlbaum.

Lundeberg, M. A., Levin, B. B., &
Harrington, H. L. (1999). *Who learns
what from cases and how? The research base
for teaching with cases.* Mahwah, NJ:
Lawrence Erlbaum.

Lynn, L. E., Jr. (1999). *Teaching and learning
with cases: A guidebook.* New York:
Chatham House.

Mauffette-Leenders, L. A., Erskine, J. A., &
Leenders, M. R. (1997). *Learning with
cases.* London, ONT: Ivey Publishing,
Ivey School of Business Administration,
The University of Western Ontario.

McClelland, R. W., Austin, C. D., & Este, D.
(1998). *Macro case studies in social work.*
Milwaukee: Families International.

Merseth, K. K. (1996). Cases and case meth-
ods in teacher education. In J. Sikula,
T. J. Buttery, & E. Guyton (Eds.),
Handbook of research on teacher education
(2nd ed., pp. 722–744). New York:
Simon & Schuster Macmillan.

Naumes, W., & Naumes, M. J. (1999). *The art
and craft of case writing.* Thousand Oaks,
CA: Sage.

Reitmeier, M. (2002). *Use of cases in social
work education.* Unpublished manuscript,
University of South Carolina,
Columbia.

Reynolds, B. C. (1942). *Learning and teaching
in the practice of social work.* New York:
Farrar & Rinehart.

Rivas, R. F., & Hull, G. H. (2000). *Case studies in generalist practice* (2nd ed.). Pacific
Grove, CA: Brooks/Cole.

Shulman, L. S. (1992). Toward a pedagogy of
cases. In J. Shulman (Ed.), *Case methods
in teacher education* (pp. 1–30). New York:
Teachers College Press.

Sykes, G., & Bird, T. (1992). Teacher education and the case idea. In G. Grant (Ed.),

Review of Research in Education (Vol. 18, pp. 457–521). Washington, DC: American Educational Research Association.

Towle, C. (1954). *The learner in education for the professions: As seen in education for social work.* Chicago: University of Chicago Press.

Weaver, R. A., Kowalski, T. J., & Pfaller, J. E. (1994). Case-method teaching. In K. W. Prichard & R. M. Sawyer (Eds.), *Handbook of college teaching: Theory and applications* (pp. 171–178). Westport, CT: Greenwood.

Welsh, M. F. (1999). A technique for cross-cultural case research and writing. In H. E. Klein (Ed.), *Interactive teaching and the multimedia revolution: Case method and other techniques* (pp. 3–9). Madison, WI: Omni.

Welty, W. M. (1989). Discussion method teaching: A practical guide. *To Improve the Academy, 8,* 197–216. [For a briefer version, see Welty, W. M. (1989). Discussion method teaching: How to make it work, *Change, 21*(4), 40–49.]

Wolfer, T. A. (2003). Decision cases for Christians in social work: Introduction to the special issue. *Social Work & Christianity, 30*(2), 103–116.

Wolfer, T. A., Freeman, M. L., & Rhodes, R. (2001). Developing and teaching an MSW capstone course using case methods of instruction. *Advances in Social Work, 2*(2), 156–171.

Chapter 2

Tips for Learning
from Decision Cases

TERRY A. WOLFER
T. LAINE SCALES

What you get out of reading, analyzing, and discussing a particular case depends largely on the method and thoroughness of your preparation. The following provides sequential tips regarding effective processes for reading and analyzing cases and for participating in decision case discussions. Some sections are drawn directly from a "Note to the Student" (Bruner, 1999), written by a master teacher for business students, while other sections were written for social work students specifically.

READING THE CASE

There are many ways to read cases. You can increase your reading effectiveness and efficiency by deliberately using different ways at various points in the process. From the very first reading, you can maximize your learning with a decision case by active, purposeful, and discriminating engagement. Bruner (1999) suggests:

> The very first time you read any case, look for the forest not the trees. This requires that your first reading be quick. Do not begin taking notes on the first round; instead, read the case like a magazine article. The first few paragraphs of a well-constructed case usually say something about the problem—read those carefully. Then quickly read the rest of the case,

seeking mainly a sense of the scope of the problems, and what information the case contains to help resolve them. Leaf through the exhibits, looking for what information they hold, rather than for any analytical insights. At the conclusion of the first pass, read any supporting articles or notes that your instructor may have recommended. (pp. xxiii–xxiv)

This brief, initial review of the case will quickly orient you to the situation and its overall context.

DIGGING INTO THE CASE SITUATION:
DEVELOP YOUR "AWARENESS"

Reading the case a second time will deepen your understanding, as Bruner (1999) reminds case readers:

With the broader perspective in mind, the second and more detailed reading will be more productive. The reason is that as you now encounter details, your mind will be able to organize them in some useful fashion rather than inventorying them randomly. Making linkages among case details is necessary toward solving the case. At this point you can take the notes that will set up your analysis. (p. xxiv)

While your instructor may provide questions to aid your preparation for particular cases, you can promote your own analytic skills by learning to pose and answer questions of your own. To begin this process, try to keep the following generic questions in mind:

1. Who is the protagonist in the case? Who must take action on the problem? What does he or she have at stake? What pressures is he or she under?

2. What is the field of practice? Who are the usual clientele? What is the demand for services? How are services funded? What are the professional affiliations and qualifications of staff? What services do the social workers provide?

3. What are the organizational auspices (e.g., public, private nonprofit, private for-profit), and who has primary authority in the organization? With whom does it collaborate or compete? Is the organization comparatively strong or weak? In what ways?

4. What are the organization's goals or desired outcomes? If not a social work organization, how does social work contribute to its goals? What are the primary intervention methods used by the organization or, if not a social work organization, the social workers who work for it?

5. How well has the organization performed in pursuit of its goals? How clearly does the organization identify its goals?

At the outset, this may sound rather daunting. There is *so much* to consider! Understand that thinking of these factors will become more natural and routine as you become more acquainted with the process of analyzing cases. The goal here is to develop greater awareness of fundamental and perennial issues, and a routine habit of attending to them. As Bruner suggests, awareness is an important attribute of successful practitioners.

DEVELOP EMPATHIC UNDERSTANDING

When reading the case, seek empathic understanding of the situation from the protagonist's perspective. It may be helpful to imagine yourself as a personal consultant to the social worker in the case. As such, you need to "start where the social worker is," to paraphrase an old cliché. Take account of the social worker's background, experience, skills, thoughts, biases, and emotions, and also of your own. Because the particular case dilemmas often involve these very factors, it is not possible or appropriate to simply replace the protagonist with your self in the case situation. These factors cannot be wished away. Any solution must take account of them, much as a consultant or supervisor would do in actual practice.

Having read and reread the case—to get a sense of the story, develop your awareness, and empathize with the protagonist—you are ready to begin more deliberate analysis. Analysis may begin with an initial statement of the problem but beware of simply adopting the perspective of the protagonist or other participants in the case.

DEFINING OR FORMULATING
THE PROBLEM

Defining or formulating the problem represents one of the most important and challenging aspects of case analysis and discussion.

> A common trap for many [practitioners] is to assume that the issue at hand is the real problem most worthy of their time, rather than a symptom of some larger problem that really deserves their time. (Bruner, 1999, p. xxv)

Students tend to take the "presenting problem" at face value, whether it's posed in the case by the client or the social worker protagonist, and assume that it represents the real problem.

> Students who are new to the case method tend to focus narrowly in defining problems and often overlook the influence which the larger setting has on the problem. In doing this, the student develops narrow

specialist habits, never achieving [a broader systems perspective]. It is useful and important for you to define the problem yourself, and in the process, validate the problem as suggested by the protagonist in the case. (p. xxv)

At this point in your analysis, it is also wise to define the problem tentatively. Treat your problem definition as a hypothesis to guide further analysis, a way to provide some structure for your thinking and questioning.

ANALYSIS: IDENTIFYING THE KEY ISSUES AND HOW THEY RELATE

The next, most time-consuming stage involves careful analysis of the case. There are several things to understand here. First, "case analysis is often iterative: an understanding of the big issues invites an analysis of details—then the details may restructure the big issues and invite the analysis of other details. In some cases, getting to the 'heart of the matter' will mean just such iteration" (Bruner, 1999, p. xxv).

Second, when doing analysis, mental experiments often help to develop insight. For example, if the client is a man, you might consider how the case might be different if the client were a woman. Or, if the client is a person of color, consider how the situation might differ if she or he were white. Alternately, you can sometimes determine a factor's relevance by mentally subtracting it from the case and considering whether the problem goes away. If there is still a problem, then the particular factor has limited relevance. Compare contrasting definitions of the situation offered by people in the case, and ask yourself how else it may be construed. Consider the client system and whether it could be defined differently. Brainstorm possible factors, on other system levels, that may cause or influence the situation. Identify what organizational policy may be relevant, unclear, or absent. Determine whether multiple ethical standards may be relevant. In short, play with definitions, comparisons, and contrasts.

Third, as you analyze the case, be prepared to revise your initial problem definition. Ask whether your emerging insights fit the problem definition. If not, try to redefine the problem in a way that accounts for your new insights. Redefining the problem requires that you reconsider other aspects of your analysis as well.

Fourth, understand that problem definition both guides analysis and also captures or reflects analysis. For most people, writing concise problem statements represents a major challenge. Skill in problem definition comes with practice and experience. "The best case students develop an instinct for where to devote their analysis. Economy of effort is desirable. If you have invested wisely in problem definition, economical analysis tends to follow" (Bruner, 1999, p. xxv). Carefully consider what belongs in the problem statement, versus what is important but not central to the problem, and therefore only belongs in the contextual analysis that supports it. Although these analytic processes can be tedious and time consuming, with practice you will become faster and more efficient.

PREPARE TO PARTICIPATE: TAKE A STAND

Eventually, you must shape your analysis of the situation into an argument for action.

> To develop analytical insights without making recommendations is useless to [practitioners], and drains the case study experience of some of its learning power. A stand means having a point of view about the problem, a recommendation, and an analysis to back up both of them. To prepare to take a stand, remember the words of Walt Disney: "Get a good idea and stay with it. Dog it and work at it until it's done, and done right." (Bruner, 1999, pp. xxv–xxvi)

Developing an argument for action requires courage; it represents a test of your case analysis. Often, there are many things at stake—especially for the client and social worker directly but also for the client's family members and associates and the social worker's organization, program, and coworkers. Despite these risks, you must choose how to act. In the world of practice, analysis that does not lead to action has limited value and may even be counterproductive.

Recognize, however, that if all students take stands, as they should, this will likely produce vigorous disagreements. Many students feel uncomfortable taking a stand, especially in the face of such disagreements. Having a strong desire to get along with their peers and instructors, they may downplay differences in their analysis or recommendations in order to reduce interpersonal tension. But this undermines the potential benefit of the process, for the group and also for the individual student. Without vigorous debate, the group may not consider diverse perspectives and students miss opportunities to practice introducing and defending their ideas. Developing the confidence and skill to assert yourself in group contexts will increase your effectiveness in family and group treatment settings, supervision sessions, meetings of professional teams, committees, or boards, or advocacy situations. In many situations, social workers will often agree and disagree. The case discussion process helps you practice doing so in direct and respectful ways.

THINGS TO AVOID WHILE PREPARING

When preparing for case discussions, there are several things to avoid. *Skipping or shortchanging preparation* will limit your ability to participate effectively in the discussion and, more importantly, will limit what you personally can learn from the discussion. You may find that reading decision cases for comprehension requires more careful and focused reading than you typically do with textbooks.

Endorsing the presenting problem may seriously bias your analysis of the case, while *ignoring the presenting problem* reflects a failure to understand an important perspective in the case. *Focusing on either details or the big picture,* to the exclusion of the other, undermines your analysis. *Jumping to conclusions* without adequate evidence prematurely ends your analysis and risks gross misunderstanding of the case. On the other hand, *not drawing conclusions* about the problem and its resolution circumvents the challenge and purpose of decision cases, reducing the opportunity to exercise and develop your decision-making skills.

ACTIVELY SUPPORT YOUR CONCLUSIONS IN THE DISCUSSION, BUT STAY OPEN TO EMERGING INSIGHTS

As a result of preparing, you may come to the discussion having already formulated conclusions, sometimes very firm conclusions, about the nature of the problem and appropriate responses. Sharing your conclusions can benefit both you and your classmates but you must remain open to their conclusions and further insights that will emerge in the discussion.

> Of course, one can have a stand without the world being any wiser. To take a stand in case discussions means to participate actively in the discussion and to advocate your stand until new facts or analysis emerge to warrant a change. Learning by the case method is not a spectator sport. A classic error many students make is to bring into the case method classroom the habits of the lecture hall (i.e., passively absorbing what other people say). These habits fail miserably in the case method classroom because they only guarantee that one absorbs the truths and fallacies uttered by others. The purpose of [decision case method] is to develop and exercise one's own skills and judgment. This takes practice and participation, just as in a sport. Here are two good general suggestions: (1) defer significant note-taking until after class and (2) strive to contribute to every case discussion. (Bruner, 1999, p. xxvi)

In short, active participation is critical for your learning. But thoughtful responding to new insights, whether these come from you or other participants, will be important, too.

LISTEN CAREFULLY

Because considering what others contribute is so important, effective participation in case discussion also requires that you listen carefully and actively. Concentrate on what others say, and on what they mean. Focus on their explicit content but also try to discern their underlying assumptions and values.

The active listening skills you may have learned for social work practice can apply in the case discussion, too. You must gain adequate understanding, through careful listening, before you can make a fair evaluation. But do evaluate what you hear, comparing it with your own ideas. Do you agree? Why or why not? (Mauffette-Leenders, Erskine, & Leenders, 1998, p. 94). At the same time, guard against focusing on what you will say next because that undermines your ability to listen effectively.

MAKING CONTRIBUTIONS

During the case discussion, students may make either content contributions or process contributions (Mauffette-Leenders et al., 1998). Content contributions include separating facts from opinions, providing analysis, identifying reasonable assumptions, or offering an action plan. An example of a content contribution would be "The immediate issue is . . . and the basic issue is . . ." (p. 86). Process contributions, in contrast, refer to the structure of the discussion. They require careful listening and observation of how the discussion unfolds. Process contributions include clarifying questions, suggesting that a certain area of the case needs to be explored further, linking points raised earlier, or summarizing the discussion thus far. An example of a process contribution would be "We need to spend more (or less) time on . . ." or "We should hear from Harry because . . ." (p. 86). You may recognize that process contributions are similar to comments an instructor or group facilitator makes. Ideally, you will learn to make both content and process contributions and also learn to recognize when either would be most appropriate and helpful. As you practice thinking like a social worker, you are practicing roles as an active member of a task group, or even as the facilitator. The point here is to contribute in various ways that move the discussion forward.

THINGS TO AVOID IN CASE DISCUSSIONS

When participating in case discussions, there are several things to avoid (Mauffette-Leenders et al., 1998, pp. 89–90). For example, *simply repeating case facts* contributes little to the discussion unless there is some confusion about the facts. *Repeating someone else's comments* reflects a failure to pay attention. *Inconsequential interjections* such as saying, "I agree," without explaining why contribute very little to the discussion. Likewise, *asking questions that divert the discussion* such as asking the instructor for his or her opinion may only delay or derail the discussion. Other *digressions* include irrelevant or out of place comments such as personal anecdotes that have little relevance to the situation. *Monopolizing the discussion* reflects an unwillingness to listen and learn from others. Sometimes students believe they have special understanding of case situations because of previous experience, and they actually do. Nevertheless, their understanding may be limited and biased by those insider perspectives. In such cases, they may benefit from the comments and questions of others having less experience. In sharp contrast, *disengaged* students rarely contribute to the discussion or, when they do jump in, tend to make superficial or irrelevant comments. Finally, *uncivil behavior* such as attacking, ridiculing, or putting down other participants or their views can have a damaging effect on case discussions.

Though in different ways, students exhibiting dominant, disengaged, and uncivil behavior all limit the diversity of viewpoints available in a discussion. Dominating behavior limits the opportunities others have to participate, while uncivil behavior may frighten and discourage others from participating. Disengaged students simply withhold their own contributions.

TRUST THE PROCESS

Case discussions may be complex, unpredictable, and bewildering. As a result, you may wonder at times where a particular discussion is headed or what you are gaining from the process. Bruner (1999) offers some good advice:

> The learnings from a case-method course are impressive. They arrive cumulatively over time. In many cases, the learnings continue well after the course has finished. Occasionally, these learnings hit you with the force of a tsunami. But generally, the learnings creep in quietly, but powerfully, like the tide. After the case course, you will look back and see that your thinking, mastery, and appreciation for [social work] have changed dramatically. The key point is that you should not measure the success of your progress on the basis of any single case discussion. Trust that in the cumulative work over many cases you will gain the mastery you seek. (p. xxvi)

With that in mind, you can hopefully maintain the kind of openness and engagement that contributes most to your learning and growth.

FOCUS ON HERE-AND-NOW PROCESS, AND RESULTS WILL FOLLOW

Bruner (1999) reminds us that the case method helps you develop and practice new ways of learning and thinking:

> View the case method experience as a series of opportunities to test your mastery of techniques and your [professional] judgment. If you seek a list of axioms to be etched in stone, you are bound to disappoint yourself. As in real life, there are virtually no "right" answers to these cases in the sense that a scientific or engineering problem has an exact solution. Jeff Milman

has said, "The answers worth getting are never found in the back of the book." What matters is that you obtain a way of thinking about [social work] situations that you can carry from one job (or career) to the next. In the case method it is largely true that how you learn is what you learn. (Bruner, 1999, p. xxvi)

MAINTAIN PERSPECTIVE

Because case method learning may be quite different from what you've experienced before, it's helpful to know that you may respond with strong emotions. These emotions may stem from unfamiliarity with the method and uncertainty about what to expect and how to participate, the unsettling nature of some case dilemmas, profound differences and conflicts that emerge in the case discussions, and the ambiguity of solutions and their likely consequences.

FINALLY, FOCUS ON
LONG-TERM OUTCOMES

At the same time, remember the learning outcomes identified in the previous chapter. These outcomes of case method learning can be quite significant overall, but less obvious for individual cases. In fact, the specific content you learn from a particular case may seem to have little value for you personally and professionally. But even when cases seem irrelevant, you can still gain experience in understanding and resolving novel situations. It's the *process* of analyzing the situation, more than the situation itself, that generates the learning. The case analyses and case discussions can help develop and refine your abilities for analyzing and resolving difficult situations. And that is good practice for learning to think like a social worker, and for the world of practice.

REFERENCES

Bruner, R. F. (1999). Note to the student: How to study and discuss cases. In *Case studies in finance: Managing for corporate value creation* (3rd ed.; pp. xxiii–xxvi). Boston: Irwin McGraw-Hill. [Also available online at http://faculty.darden.virginia.edu/brunerb/resources_studentnote.htm]

Mauffette-Leenders, L. A., Erskine, J. A., & Leenders, M. R. (1998). *Learning with cases.* London, ONT: Ivey Publishing, Ivey School of Business Administration, The University of Western Ontario.

PART II

Cases

Case 1

Jim's License to Drive[1]

KAREN A. GRAY
TERRY A. WOLFER

Standing on the street corner, the November evening air was chilly. But to Jim Miller, social work student and agency director, the reception felt colder. Facing him, some 20 Latino men crossed their arms and lowered their faces, and some turned to walk away. Jim could feel the trust being sucked away. Without asking, Jim knew they felt he had let them down.

Jim had had such high hopes for The Friendship Center, the community center that he helped found. Now it seemed to be crumbling around him, and he wondered if any of his efforts were salvageable. *What, if anything, can I do to keep the center alive? My word is no longer good,* he thought to himself.

JIM MILLER

Jim Miller was a first year MSW student when, in fall 2001, he began a field placement at a teen pregnancy program in Monroe, North Carolina. Because he was bilingual, speaking both English and Spanish, he was constantly asked

1. Development of this decision case was supported in part by funding from the University of South Carolina College of Social Work. It was prepared solely to provide material for class discussion and not to suggest either effective or ineffective handling of the situation depicted. While based on field research regarding an actual situation, names and certain facts may have been disguised to protect confidentiality. The author and editors wish to thank the anonymous case reporter for his cooperation in making this account available for the benefit of social work students and instructors. Revised from an appendix in Gray, K. A., Wolfer, T. A., & Maas, C. (forthcoming). Using decision case method to teach grassroots community organizing. *Journal of Community Practice.* Article copies available from the Haworth Document Delivery Service: 1-800-HAWORTH. E-mail address: docdelivery@haworthpress.com. Copyright © 2005 Haworth Press.

to interpret both in and outside the agency. As a result, he met many community members and, as he later recalled, he "inadvertently became a voice for the [Latino] community."

Jim came to the MSW program with several years of macro-type experience. After obtaining his undergraduate degree, Jim worked as a community development specialist for 2 years. Then, he worked for 3 years as a Women In Development Coordinator in Small Project Assistance programming with the Peace Corps and USAID in Ecuador. He also worked one year for the North Carolina Department of Juvenile Justice and Delinquency Prevention (DJJDP) and another year in a Job Training Partnership Act (JTPA) program.

The many social injustices Jim had observed while working motivated his return to school. He clearly had the "fire in the belly" that activists say is required to do community organizing or other activist work; he felt passionate about fighting oppression. As an Anglo man, he had learned to be culturally sensitive in his international work. This, combined with his intelligence and his fluency in Spanish, meant he brought important assets to practice. During his first year in Monroe, Jim developed good relationships with various community groups, agencies, and politicians. Initially, many in this small Southern town were suspicious of him. Because he was an outsider who became involved with the recent Latino population, Jim continually had to assure people that he had no intentions of organizing the Latino population for union membership. Soon enough, people trusted him, and he was invited by a community liaison at the local hospital to sit on the Latino immigrant health task force. The task force obtained grant money to conduct a health survey and the results suggested that there were a wide variety of untreated health needs. Further, the task force learned that Latinos in Monroe were not receiving adequate health care for a number of reasons, including social isolation, and financial and language barriers. The task force had grant money left over from the implementation of the survey and decided to give Jim $8,000 to start a community center. The original purpose of the community center was to provide health services.

As a result, while still a first year MSW student, Jim served as the founding director of The Friendship Center. Jim did not lack for things to do. In addition to his responsibility as director, Jim juggled the usual classes, a two-day field placement, and a one-day graduate assistantship at the university.

Jim's personal investments in the community surrounding The Friendship Center were complex and multifaceted. Because he was bilingual, the police frequently called Jim to interpret for Spanish-speaking community members who were under arrest. As a student, he used community data for a research project and wrote papers about the community. He presented this research and two papers at several statewide conferences. He felt that the community gave him a great deal, and he felt obligated to return the favors.

He also hoped that the Latino community would gain a voice. Whether or not the Latinos who resided in Monroe had the proper documents, Jim believed strongly that they did not deserve deplorable working conditions nor to be taken advantage of by unscrupulous employers. They had basic human rights. And they were contributing members of the community. His ultimate dream was to build an environment where children could prosper and be safe.

THE "NEW JACK CITY" COMMUNITY

The community surrounding The Friendship Center was nicknamed "New Jack City," or simply "New Jack," by people living outside the community. Locally, New Jack was famous for being the first neighborhood in Monroe to have drive-by shootings, crack dealers, and gang activity. For more than a decade, it had been considered a dangerous place to live, work, or simply pass through.

The composition of the community had changed dramatically in the last 2 years. While it used to be 100 percent African American, it was now 80 percent Latino. A labor contractor recruited the Latinos to work at Wilson's, the local chicken processing plant, in low-wage, low-skill jobs.

When Jim arrived in Monroe, racial tensions were running high. Most of the workers who were fired from Wilson's over the previous 2 years were African American. Most of the replacement workers were Latino because, as the Wilson CEO allegedly claimed, "The workers we had before were addled with drugs and they were an unreliable labor force. They were unable to meet our production demands. We were at the brink of closing the plant." The CEO was quick to explain that Wilson's didn't hire the Latinos, but simply contracted with Key Employment, a labor contractor.

Key Employment had contracts all over North Carolina. Its owner, Bob Slusser, hired a *coyote* to recruit and transport potential workers from Mexico. Bob also set up a pyramid system to run his business. He hired Latino *contratistas*, like Antonio Cruz, to supervise. In exchange for arranging and supervising employment, a *contratista* took a cut of the worker's pay (typically $1 per hour) and Bob took a cut, too (another $1 per hour).

In Monroe, many members of the Latino community worked at Wilson's, where they earned $7.50 per hour (before the withholdings noted above). They often worked 6 days per week. Wilson's paid rent and utilities for the workers to live in some rundown apartments in New Jack, and they paid Antonio to manage the apartment complex. Although Wilson's paid the rent, workers had to buy their own work supplies, such as boots.

Wilson's was located within walking distance of New Jack, so people had no problem getting to work. But because there was no public transportation in Monroe, and because cabs were expensive, owning a car or carpooling were the only reasonable means of transportation to the grocery store and church. But getting a license posed a particular problem for the Latinos, as most were undocumented. As a result, they just drove without licenses. Driving without a license might not have caught so much attention except for an elevated rate of DUIs within Monroe's Latino community.

Latinos arrested for driving without a license and without automobile insurance were typically fined $800 and jailed until they could pay the fine or a bond. If arrested for DUI, the penalties were even stiffer. In any case, because they received low wages, the Latinos found it nearly impossible to pay these fines and get out of jail. And most did not have family members nearby who could help them out.

But the Latinos had more serious legal concerns. Because most did not have the proper documents, they were always looking over their shoulders for *la migra*. In 1997, the INS deported 172 people from another community with a Wilson's chicken processing plant. The Latinos believed that Wilson's made the call to INS because workers were beginning to organize a union.

THE FRIENDSHIP CENTER

"With the $8,000," Jim recalled, "we rented an apartment in the neighborhood and BOOM! we started going. We just did whatever we could get together, with mostly in-kind resources." But he soon secured new funding from several sources, mostly from a local, private foundation.

The initial mission of the center was fourfold: (1) English as a Second Language (ESL) classes, (2) after-school and other children's activities, (3) monthly health screenings, including pap smears, and (4) community development.

Instead of a board of directors, the center had an advisory board. The board chair, Jane Long, was a sociology professor from the local community college. As board chair, she was Jim's boss. Although the agencies represented at the advisory board meetings were fairly constant, different agency representatives attended the meetings. In other words, each agency was a member of the board, with representatives revolving. Typically, about 15 people attended. The number and diversity of the members were impressive. The advisory board meetings usually consisted of religious leaders, like Reverend Al Smith (who ran an anti-gang program), a chamber of commerce representative, a representative of the mayor's office, Sergeant Tom Johnson from the Monroe police department, a literacy council member, a Memorial Hospital representative, a city council representative, a parks and recreation employee, a free medical clinic employee, immigrant health task force members, the director of the Monroe county department of social services, and five core community people, like Antonio Cruz. Some had lived in New Jack for years and some were new. Jim had invited most community members face to face.

COMMUNITY MEETINGS

To fulfill the community development mission of The Friendship Center, Jim organized the first general community meeting in August 2001. It was a cook-out with Leland Jordan, the African American mayor of Monroe. Because he was dressed in shorts and cooked hot dogs and hamburgers, the Latinos didn't believe Jim when he said this was the mayor. In Latin American countries, they said, the mayor always wore a suit and tie and would never "serve" constituents by cooking.

Several weeks prior to the September community meeting, at a meeting of the advisory board, Jim mentioned his concern about the number of unlicensed drivers and DUIs in the Latino community, and wondered what prevention tactics could be set in place. As a result, Reverend Smith introduced Jim to Everett Blue, a community education specialist with the North Carolina Department of Alcohol and Substance Abuse. Everett said he had a fantastic brochure that addressed Jim's concerns, but it would need to be translated into Spanish. Jim agreed to do this. The brochure was not just about DUIs. It also explained North Carolina driving laws and how to get a driver's license—a sort of "Welcome, Neighbor" brochure that Jim thought would be a wonderful "Welcome, Neighbor from Mexico" brochure once translated into Spanish. Without waiting for permission from the state department of transportation, Jim started making copies and handing out the brochure in the community.

The brochure said that if one brought a birth certificate and picture identification card to the department of motor vehicles, and a letter from the social security office stating why a social security number could not be assigned, one could get a driver's license, even without a social security number. With this information, Antonio started translating birth certificates for $25 per person.

Jim convinced Mayor Jordan to return to the second community meeting. This was no small task. Jim knew Mayor Jordan had taken some flack from African American citizens for being "too cozy" with the Latino population. Several community leaders insisted that because he was African American, the mayor should be helping African Americans, not Latinos.

Besides getting the mayor to attend again, Jim arranged for Manuel Ramos, the owner of an unlicensed weekend restaurant, to cook his famous, delicious chicken. Latinos curious about this American mayor came to the September community meeting. At least 75 people attended to socialize and to present their concerns about their inability to obtain a driver's license. Mayor Jordan said he would talk to the police department, the social security office, and the department of motor vehicles, and find out how to get driver's licenses. He promised to report this information at the October community meeting. Naturally, this excited folks.

Before the October community meeting, Jim mentioned to Jane, "The local social security office is not providing the services it is required to provide. 'Jim Crow' is being replaced by 'Juan Crow' laws." He explained the office was supposed to provide anyone who requested a social security number either a number or a letter explaining why she or he did not qualify. Such a letter could be used to obtain a driver's license without a social security number. Instead, he reported, the director Anita Williams, an African American, posted a yellow flyer at the social security office that stated without correct papers from the INS, one could not be served by social security.

Incensed by this information, Jane took a video camera and some Latinos to the local department of motor vehicles office. She filmed an African American man in line in front of them obtaining a driver's license without producing a social security number when asked for one. When Jane and the Latinos' turn came, the Latinos were denied a license because they had no social security number.

At the October community meeting, Mayor Jordan sent a representative in his place. The representative, an African American woman, did not know anything about the driver's license issue, and therefore had nothing to report. The 40–50 Latinos at the meeting grumbled a bit, but Jim tried to appease them by saying, "This kind of thing takes time."

Jim decided to move the November community meeting to a more central part of the neighborhood, in hopes that more African American community members would show up. He selected a laundry mat parking lot. It was late on a Sunday afternoon, almost dark and quite chilly when the meeting began. Only when the meeting began, did Jim remember that the local drug dealers occupied an adjacent corner of the block.

Nevertheless, Jim was pleased to see several new African American faces in the crowd, and went to introduce himself and offer dinner. There was no famous chicken this time but the cook's famous *posole* instead. When the new attendees introduced themselves as Black Muslims, however, Jim was embarrassed that he had nothing but pork to offer them.

The other 20 people present were Latino men. Some women and children had stopped by earlier, but they appeared uncomfortable and left before Jim could extend a welcome.

Twenty minutes after the scheduled start time, Jane had not yet arrived. In addition, there was no mayor and no representative. Jim felt abandoned by his colleagues. People were getting antsy, so Jim reluctantly began the meeting alone. The Latinos wanted to know about driver's licenses but Jim had no news to give them. Facing him, the men crossed their arms and lowered their faces, the disappointment evident. Quickly, some turned to walk away. But even with those who hesitated, Jim could feel the trust being sucked away. Without asking, Jim knew they felt he had let them down.

As the meeting ended, Jim felt stumped about what to do next, and how to understand what was going wrong. He had held such high hopes for the community center that he helped found but now it seemed to be crumbling around him. Discouraging questions tumbled through his mind. *Now what? What, if anything, can I do to keep the center alive? Can we salvage any of our efforts here? Is my word any good in this community? How can I still be a community leader and regain people's trust? Do I have to suck up to the mayor? What do I do first?*

Case 2

Larry Steele's Group[1]

MELISSA C. REITMEIER
TERRY A. WOLFER

A s a contract therapist at the Domestic Abuse Institute for 2 years, Jacquelyn Ferrante had grown comfortable facilitating psychoeducational groups for men who had perpetrated domestic abuse. On a Tuesday evening in August 2001, preparing for another session, Jacquelyn quickly found her usual parking space at the church and was looking forward to getting to group early as usual to unwind and set up. She had just gotten out of her car and was gathering her things when a large black man she'd never met approached her rapidly. He was somewhat overdressed and wearing a large, shiny gold cross on a gold chain around his neck. It swayed as he made his way to Jacquelyn's car. Immediately, Jacquelyn wondered, *Who is this running toward me?* Jacquelyn felt her pulse quicken.

THE DOMESTIC ABUSE INSTITUTE

The Domestic Abuse Institute (DAI) was a private, not-for-profit corporation, founded in Richmond, Virginia, in 1982. Its purpose was to provide counseling for perpetrators of domestic abuse and violence seeking attitudinal and

1. Development of this decision case was supported in part by funding from the University of South Carolina College of Social Work. It was prepared solely to provide material for class discussion and not to suggest either effective or ineffective handling of the situation depicted. While based on field research regarding an actual situation, names and certain facts may have been disguised to protect confidentiality. The authors and editors wish to thank the anonymous case reporter for her cooperation in making this account available for the benefit of social work students and instructors. Copyright © 2005 Thomson Learning.

behavioral change. DAI started small, serving only two counties, but gradually received funds to expand its services to more areas throughout the state. It accepted court referrals of individuals who could either fulfill a mandated commitment to the program or serve prison time for their crimes related to domestic abuse.

All therapists held master's degrees and were trained in group therapy methods and domestic violence issues. DAI used a manual-based, cognitive behavioral approach to group treatment: group members were provided workbooks that outlined the concepts and skills taught in each session. Some contract therapists followed the workbook to the letter, but Jacquelyn did not. To her mind, certain parts of the workbook simply did not apply to some members of the group. Furthermore, some group participants lacked the literacy skills necessary for using the workbook. Contact between DAI and the contract therapists occurred on an "as needed" basis. No formal team consultation process was in place, yet Jacquelyn had always felt comfortable contacting her supervisor with questions or concerns.

Group counseling sessions were conducted on various nights and in various locations in counties throughout central Virginia. At intake, all participants attended two sessions in which staff provided psychological testing and information on group dynamics and expectations. Then group counseling was offered on a weekly basis in a small group setting, twelve 90-minute psychoeducational sessions for concepts and skills acquisition and then another twelve 90-minute process-oriented sessions for applying skills learned the previous twelve weeks. The psychoeducational approach differed from traditional therapy in that it emphasized teaching specific skills and focused on applying these skills in the here and now. Little time was spent on exploring the reasons for past behaviors.

Group members were required to finish 24 weeks of therapy to complete the mandated program. When clients completed the program, DAI provided a written report concerning their participation to the referring judge or agency for review and final determination. Members who did not complete the program successfully went back to court to have the judge decide how their cases should be handled.

Groups were flexibly structured. The groups were open-ended; new members could join at any time and continue until they completed the two 12-week modules. Reading levels, ethnicity, age, and socioeconomic status varied within groups. New intakes could pick which group to attend based on group time and location. There was a wide range of choices, with groups meeting every weeknight except Friday and several times on Saturday morning.

Group members' violations ranged from yelling at spouses or others in the home to serious physical assaults. Often, the general public referred to members of these groups as "batterers." However, Jacquelyn avoided this description. She preferred that people refer to these individuals as perpetrators of domestic violence.

JACQUELYN FERRANTE

Prior to earning an MSW degree at Virginia Commonwealth University, Jacquelyn Ferrante, a 56-year-old Southern, white woman, had had a very successful 16-year career as an editor and writer. For several years before that she'd been a stay-at-home mom. Because she wanted a deeper understanding of the social implications of some of her work, she decided to pursue her master's degree in social work. Jacquelyn had grown up with a lot of men around, so it was not surprising that she would take an interest in serious social issues affecting men. After considering volunteering for a women's abuse group and having that fall through, Jacquelyn thought, *Hey, it would be interesting to see what the other side of the equation is.* She soon began volunteering at DAI, as a student in training, to get some experience in working with men who perpetrated domestic abuse. Jacquelyn knew right away she had found her niche and was excited about working with this population. As soon as she got her social work state license several months after graduation, she asked to run psychoeducational groups for DAI. Doug Brady, DAI's executive director, remembered Jacquelyn and was pleased to employ her as a contract therapist. Jacquelyn ran one group per week for DAI. Although Jacquelyn wanted to continue her work with men, she also worked a full-time job at a research and training center.

Although Jacquelyn was only 5 feet tall and weighed 95 pounds, she had a powerful presence. She had always encouraged and demanded respect for group members and the group process. Her clients often told her that when they first saw her, they thought, "Here's another woman to screw me over." Jacquelyn handled such comments with aplomb, typically responding, "It makes sense why you might feel that way." She often encouraged members to explore their feelings behind the thoughts, "What emotions are you experiencing, right now? Let's discuss it." As a result, the men in her group had little problem conveying what they really thought.

JACQUELYN'S GROUP
COUNSELING SESSIONS

Jacquelyn held her group at St. Peter's, an old Catholic church, in a small town about 30 miles from Richmond. Two other counseling groups met there at the same time: another men's group and a group for women perpetrators of domestic abuse. Maroon carpeting and dimly lit sconces filled the church corridors, and handmade signs guided group members to the group meeting rooms. Because St. Peter's hosted several community activities simultaneously, Jacquelyn's group met in the church's nursery. To create a space conducive for group process, she simply arranged adult-size folding chairs in a circle where members could gather, learn skills, and share stories.

Jacquelyn's group typically included up to 12 men, aged 18–50, nearly all white. Jacquelyn never knew who or how many might be coming to group. Sometimes men from other groups would visit her group to make up for a class they couldn't attend for some reason or would stay in her group beyond the initial 12 weeks of psychoeducational skills if the nearest therapy groups were too full for them to join for the remaining 12 weeks.

Jacquelyn was never quite sure of an individual's medical or mental health history because DAI rarely sent her the completed intake evaluations before clients began the mandated course of treatment. Furthermore, the contract therapists were not involved in the 2 days of intake and orientation and had little knowledge about their clients' mental or medical health unless the clients themselves offered or disclosed information during group sessions. Initially Jacquelyn had made more of an effort to get the intake evaluations ahead of time, but she had finally concluded that they weren't all that significant. They rarely, if ever, resulted in anyone's exclusion from group. For example, once she'd gotten an evaluation with "Red Alert" written at the top, several weeks after a group member had been a part of group. When she inquired what this meant, Doug Brady had said, "This guy has a high propensity for anger and violence." Sure enough, the client was very angry; but he had been doing quite well in Jacquelyn's group.

Although Doug advised the therapists that he was available if they had concerns or questions, he typically took a "hands off" approach to supervision. Jacquelyn never knew how to read his behaviors when she sought supervision.

A NEW MEMBER

Jacquelyn had been running a group for 2 years when an unfamiliar African American man approached her in the parking lot before a group session. As he approached, Jacquelyn wondered, *Is this guy attending my group? He doesn't look like the other group members: besides, they never approach me. But if not, then who is he?*

Taken aback by his approach, Jacquelyn asked, "Are you in my group?"

"Why, yes, I am, if you're Mrs. Fairing. My name is Larry, Larry Steele." Forging ahead, Larry volunteered bits of his personal history in a sequence that seemed disconnected to Jacquelyn. A bit overwhelmed by all this information, she made her way to the front of the church to go in and set up for group. As she walked, she turned to Larry and said, "You can come through the church with me, but after tonight you need to go through the back door."

Once they got inside the large outer doors, she led him through a hallway to open the back door to the nursery, where the group members usually entered. Larry followed, chattering the whole way. When Jacquelyn proceeded to set up the chairs and arrange the room, Larry volunteered to help. Because he was present and talking nonstop, she missed the usual opportunity to unwind and focus on the upcoming group session.

At the beginning of group, Jacquelyn started with a "check-in." Every member got an opportunity to say how their week had gone, and new members introduced themselves and shared their stories. During check-in, Larry repeated to the group essentially what he had said to Jacquelyn earlier.

"I'm well known in my community. Believe me, people would recognize me if I went to a group there. So I came out here instead. I've had a lot of things happen to me in my life—lost both my parents early, and my grandmother took all us children in. I've lost some of my siblings and a lot of friends, been in and out of mental institutions—I was diagnosed schizophrenic when I was 18. Some bad things have happened to me, and what happened with my wife was another one. But I'll get through this . . ."

As he rambled on, Jacquelyn thought, *He's sharing too much, talking too much. And he wants to look great to the other group members. I wonder if he's going to be able to open himself up to this experience enough to get anything from it. Worse, will he keep others from doing their personal work? But poor guy . . . he hasn't had a lot of chances in his life.*

At check-in the next week, Larry began, "Say, did you know that women are the cause of all the evils and problems in the world?" He was smiling, and his eyes moved to take in the whole circle as he spoke. "It goes back to the Garden of Eden, when Eve tempted Adam with the apple. And ever since then. . . ."

The others looked at Jacquelyn to see how she'd respond. Trying to keep the annoyance from showing on her face, Jacquelyn was thinking, *How do I deal with this? From the point of view of respect for women? He's not going to go for the story-as-metaphor approach, for sure. That gold cross he was wearing last week is something more than jewelry to this flaming fundamentalist.* Some of the men were snickering by this point, but a few were sitting straighter in their chairs, facial muscles tightened and lips in a straight line. For a moment, Jacquelyn wondered, *Does this kind of behavior justify his removal?* Then she told herself, *It's probably not severe enough. I'll just ignore it for now. Maybe he will "get it" after another week.*

By the third week, Jacquelyn began to wonder seriously what she should do about Larry. Out of the blue, Larry said, "If my son ever told me he was a homosexual, I would beat the hell out of him." He followed this statement up with some quotes from the Bible.

Jacquelyn responded by saying, "There will be respect in this room and respect for others' way of life." She kept thinking to herself, *He's had such a hard life; I don't want to add to his pain by recommending that he be taken out of the group. I hope he'll get it. Everything will be okay, if I just wait. Besides, by the fourth week most people have settled down enough to relax and give others a chance to talk.*

Thoughts of Larry's behaviors and her responses kept replaying in Jacquelyn's head as she drove home that evening. Jacquelyn tried to sort out why this man provoked such a strong reaction in her. She thought, *I hate this guy.* And her immediate next thought was, *What does this say about me as a therapist? How can I help this man?* She was shocked at how unprofessional she felt. Jacquelyn told herself, *Perhaps I should talk to Larry before the next meeting and ask him how we can address his behaviors.*

Before group session on the fifth week, two planes crashed into the twin towers in New York City. Thousands of people were thought dead and the nation was in shock. Due to the circumstances, Jacquelyn decided she would use group time to allow members the opportunity to talk about what had happened that day and how the group members were feeling about it. At the same time, she realized there might be some who didn't feel like talking or would rather be with their families or friends elsewhere. People responded differently to tragedy, so she offered, "If any of you want to be somewhere else for any reason, you can leave and still be counted present for the week."

When Larry wanted to lead the group in prayer, Jacquelyn responded, "This is not a religious group."

Larry glowered at her. "We're meeting in a church!" he countered, "And besides, it's the *right* thing to do."

After asking the other group members whether they had any objections, Jacquelyn gave Larry permission to lead the group in prayer.

Speaking firmly, Larry instructed the others to stand, clasp hands in the circle, and close their eyes. He offered a prayer and, without inviting others to pray, said, "Amen."

After asking Jacquelyn if she really meant they could leave, Larry left immediately.

The only other person who left was a young man whose father had been scheduled for a 9 A.M. meeting at the World Trade Center. The young man had not heard from his father. He left only after Jacquelyn urged him to go and be with his mother in case they got some news.

THE BRUCE CYCLONE

At Larry's sixth group meeting, a newer member diverted Jacquelyn's attention. A white man in his 30s, Bruce Stone had come to group 2 weeks earlier, bringing a lot of resentment with him. To Jacquelyn, his intense blue eyes seemed almost sinister. He often sat rigid in his chair, with arms folded, glaring at the group. At check-in, he usually started by declaring, "This group sucks."

This particular week, the group had a good rhythm going at check-in when Bruce sauntered in 14 minutes late, one minute short of the grace period to be counted present for the week. When Bruce entered the room, the group members sat up and took notice—even Larry. Jacquelyn thought, *Bruce is trying to be the leader of the pack, to undermine the men's loyalty to group.* Several group members checked their watches and glanced at Jacquelyn for her response. Bruce announced, "I got something I want to share."

Surprised that he would interrupt the process, Jacquelyn replied, "Well, take a seat, Bruce, and you can share when it's your turn."

Bruce picked a chair two seats away from Jacquelyn and pushed it back, out of the circle. He positioned his body so that Jacquelyn could not see his face.

When Bruce's turn came, Jacqueline asked him, "What would you like to share?"

"This group sucks, and I think you're all losers." Bruce burst out, looking directly at Larry.

Calmly, Jacquelyn probed, "Well, why do you feel this way?"

Looking through Jacquelyn with those bright blue eyes, Bruce continued, "Cause you're a loser and this group sucks!" Then looking at Larry, he announced, "You piss me off, you and your sweetie-sweet comments to the others and always saying how well you're doing and how you've changed and you've gotten a grip on your anger and . . . ."

As the torrent of words flowed, Larry rose to address Bruce, "Don't tell me I'm a loser! You don't know me. You don't know what it's been like for me. I have tried real hard to get my life together. At least I am willing. I put forth an effort to learn in group. You don't do jack shit!"

Bruce rose to respond, his muscular 6-foot frame towering over Larry, and retorted, "You don't know what I do or what I try." Bruce scanned each group member's face, searching, and then he emphasized, "None of you have got a fucking clue!"

Another man rose to join the verbal fray, and words started flying between the three standing group members.

Jacquelyn watched as the tension grew in the group: faces twisting, bodies tensing, and clients squirming in their seats. Respect was the keynote of Jacquelyn's group; she was sure all the men knew this. The third man's hands had become fists. With even more concern she looked back to Bruce and Larry. She thought, *There could be a fight here, and how in the world am I going to stop it? But somehow I have to.*

Jacquelyn rose out of her chair and said firmly, "Stop it! Just stop it. There will not be disrespect in this group, so everybody sit down. We're going to continue with what we were doing before this all started." Pausing momentarily, "Bruce, I want you to keep quiet during the rest of the meeting. Later we'll talk about what this means for you in group. I'll have to think about that and discuss with DAI what's happened and what we need to do about it."

The next day Jacquelyn called Doug and told him of the disruption in the group. Doug shared Jacquelyn's concern and decided to remove Bruce from the group.

DECISION TIME

DAI had no specific policy for removing members. It was up to the therapists and the executive director to determine what behaviors warranted removal and reappearance before the court. During the 2 years Jacquelyn had run groups for DAI, she had only recommended removal of three clients, including Bruce. Those instances each seemed more serious than the current situation with Larry. However, Jacquelyn thought that Larry dominated the group and disturbed the other group members. She wondered whether she should recommend that Larry leave the group, too. Jacquelyn thought to herself, *He is open and sincere, and even seems motivated to learn. But he is consistently judgmental of other group members. He waits for me before group sessions, wants control of group itself, and wants to talk to me after group—he knows the answers to everything. He just won't let up.*

A week after the Bruce incident, Larry mentioned that his daughter had asked to go to a certain upcoming concert and said that he'd told her no, that he didn't approve. Danny, a teenager in the group, said, "That concert would be OK—the singer's a decent guy, not into profanity or putting down women or authority figures. Besides," the teen said, "if you just automatically tell your daughter she can't do certain things, no discussion, it will only be a matter of time before she does them behind your back."

Larry lit into the young man. "You don't have kids! What do you know? You've gotten into it with your own father." Then, with contempt, "Don't tell me how to raise my kids!"

Jacquelyn intervened immediately. "Do you remember what we've said about respect? Do you remember what happened just last week? Danny has listened to your opinion on many things, and he has a right to express his opinion and be heard."

That evening on the way home, Jacquelyn wondered, *Should I have recommended removing Larry from group a long time ago? It almost seems unjust to do it at this point, but still, there are other group members to consider. Things don't seem to be getting any better.*

Case 3

Advocating for Clients[1]

JEANETTE UCCI
TERRY A. WOLFER

It seemed to Alice Summer that she and Ted Jakes, Director of South Carolina Department of Social Services (SCDSS), had truly reached an impasse. She firmly believed that her views were correct and that she was trying to safeguard the well being of the DSS clients. She and a coworker decided that their best plan would be to pitch their opinion to Jakes in one last attempt at convincing him to follow their plans. Together they prepared their arguments, and sat down to meet with him.

"You know, the statewide training meetings are going to begin soon," Summer began, well aware of the tense atmosphere in the room. "My colleagues and I are planning to train the directors as if there will be one worker, not two."

Jakes looked skeptical, but did not say anything, so Summer continued.

"I've been working here for 15 years, and I know caseworkers. I believe you're wrong. Trust me on this, our plan is the way to go," she said.

1. Development of this decision case was supported in part by funding from the University of South Carolina College of Social Work. It was prepared solely to provide material for class discussion and not to suggest either effective or ineffective handling of the situation depicted. While based on field research regarding an actual situation, names and certain facts may have been disguised to protect confidentiality. The authors and editors wish to thank the anonymous case reporter for her cooperation in making this account available for the benefit of social work students and instructors. Copyright © 2005 Thomson Learning.

An uncomfortable pause followed. Then Jakes responded, "No, I don't think your plan will work. And besides," he continued, "if I choose to implement your plan, and it fails, as I believe it would, you will be held accountable. It will be on your head."

Summer and her coworker sat for a moment in silence, absorbing what Jakes had just said. *Where do we go from here*, she wondered to herself.

A CHANGING POLITICAL CONTEXT

In 1994, South Carolina elected Republican David Beasley as governor. He replaced a popular two-term Republican, Carroll Campbell, and defeated the Democratic candidate, Nick Theodore. Beasley had made welfare reform a key component of his campaign. His focus on this issue reflected the early stages of an emerging national trend of welfare reform. Beasley had made it well known during his campaign that he intended to place a particular emphasis on making changes to the Aid to Families with Dependent Children (AFDC) program that SCDSS administered. He held the belief that receiving AFDC benefits fostered dependency in the recipients, instead of assisting them to achieve economic self-sufficiency. Beasley's intense focus on making changes in DSS services had a personal basis, as he related during his campaign. His mother had worked as a DSS caseworker, and he retained vivid memories of her stories about the economic situations of her clients. In particular, Beasley pointed toward young teen mothers with children, stating that these women were using AFDC benefits to establish their own households and families. One of his campaign slogans had been "Stop paying children to have children." As a result, Beasley's campaign and election promised greater than usual scrutiny for SCDSS.

SOUTH CAROLINA DEPARTMENT
OF SOCIAL SERVICES

Headquartered in Columbia, SCDSS carried responsibility for administering a large and complex set of federal and state social welfare programs, many more than the child welfare and AFDC programs for which it was best known. Statewide, SCDSS administered 46 county offices and employed nearly 5,000 staff members. The agency director was appointed by and served at the pleasure of the governor, part of a cabinet form of government.

The SCDSS defined its mission as: "To ensure the health and safety of children and adults who cannot protect themselves, to help parents and caregivers provide nurturing homes, and to help people in need of financial assistance reach their highest level of social and economic self-sufficiency. The agency's goal is to help people live better lives" (SCDSS, n.d.).

SCDSS services were grouped under four main offices, each of which included several divisions.

1. The Office of County Operations supervised day-to-day activities for each of the 46 county offices, out of which direct service employees implemented programs. Included under the Office of County Operations were the Divisions of Information Resource Management, Program Quality Assurance, Regional Administrators, Staff Development and Training, and County Technical Support Staff.

2. The Office of Administration handled contracts, hiring and firing personnel, and programmatic appeals. It included the Divisions of Community Resources, Departmental Services, Individual and Provider Rights, Ombudsman/Client Inquiry, and Personnel.

3. The Office of Fiscal Management developed budgets for all agency programs. Included under this office were the three divisions of Budgeting, Cost Allocation Systems, and Finance.

4. The Office of Program Policy and Oversight developed and disseminated policies for all of the SCDSS programs administered statewide. It also interpreted federal policies. In 1995, the Office of Program Policy and Oversight included six divisions. The Division of Adult Services provided case management assistance to vulnerable adults, while the Division of Child Day Care Licensing and Regulatory Services was responsible for licensing childcare programs throughout the state. The Division of Child Support Enforcement administered programs to locate parents, establish paternity, and secure and enforce child support orders. The Division of Family Preservation and Child Welfare Services included Child Protective Services, Foster Care, and Adoption. The Division of Medical Support was responsible for determining people's eligibility for Medicaid throughout South Carolina. Finally, the Division of Policy and Planning developed and disseminated policies for welfare and food stamp programs.

As a large and complex organization, SCDSS could not change easily or quickly. But by the nature of its mission and clientele, it was also often a lightening rod for public controversy.

DIRECTOR TED JAKES

As suggested by his campaign, following his inauguration Beasley took special interest in several state agencies, particularly SCDSS. Though his was a continuing Republican administration, Beasley appointed several new directors of state agencies, including Ted Jakes at SCDSS.

Ted Jakes brought with him a great deal of experience with welfare reform in the State of Florida. Because of his campaign's emphasis on welfare reform, Governor Beasley sought an SCDSS director who clearly shared his beliefs regarding welfare, who could work quickly and efficiently, and who was likely to have some immediate large-scale successes. For his part, Jakes held Beasley's expectations for job performance in high regard. Jakes's primary focus was on welfare reform, and he had an impressive knowledge of policy and procedures. Based on his previous work with welfare reform in Florida, Jakes entered SCDSS armed with a supply of energy, commitment, and new ideas.

Jakes's new ideas often puzzled long-time staff members, and many of them thought his proposals were quite strange. For example, Jakes thought that some of the individual county-level DSS offices should be consolidated, that having one in every county was unnecessary duplication of services. He also supported privatizing some of the functions that DSS workers carried out, that is, subcontracting selected services to businesspeople to improve efficiency. Furthermore, Jakes believed that AFDC and food stamp benefits should be administered through block grants, not through open funding, as was the case in 1995. At the time, this belief was "revolutionary," and many DSS staff members found it "very scary." Perhaps most significantly, Jakes had high expectations for his clients: he was convinced that most welfare families were able to work. His viewpoints differed fundamentally from the long-held underpinnings of existing welfare programs and many staff at DSS had never questioned the way programs were run. Once Jakes had an opportunity to explain his ideas, however, staff often thought they seemed more reasonable.

Jakes's leadership style also represented a major change for the employees he supervised. Previously, the director of SCDSS had little involvement with the actual day-to-day work of particular SCDSS programs. But because Beasley had appointed Jakes for his wealth of experience with welfare reform, Jakes made certain that he took a very active role with the Office of Program Policy and Oversight. Unlike some previous directors, he was a very visible leader, and apparently knew a great deal about welfare policy. Jakes's behavior conveyed the message, "make no mistake about it, I will be intimately involved" in all aspects of economic assistance policy.

Newly appointed and with a clear vision, Jakes was very excited about leading welfare reform at SCDSS. To begin, he solicited reports from staff members on their previous and current efforts related to welfare reform. He reviewed the paperwork and listened to what they had done. Sometimes, when reviewing their efforts, he replied, "Okay, we're not doing that." Other times, he would push to broaden and speed up small demonstration projects beyond a few counties, saying, "Whatever we do, we are going to do statewide, and we need to get to work on this right away, because the governor wants this legislation introduced in late January, or in early February at the latest."

When Jakes began as director, his extreme intelligence and imposing physical presence often intimidated employees at the agency, even leading some to perceive him as arrogant. When he reviewed a draft that an employee had written, he typically returned it with comments and recommended changes longer than the original draft. Nevertheless, as a leader, Jakes set very clear goals and consistently reminded his staff of these goals. He also set strict deadlines for projects and insisted that they be met. From Summer's perspective, Jakes was a caring person who was sincere about his beliefs and thoroughly committed to improving client services.

Jakes also placed a high emphasis on accountability. This was true of his views of both the SCDSS employees and their clients. His approach toward his subordinates was almost managerial in nature, reflecting his businesslike approach toward supervision. In his eyes, the best way to motivate workers and clients to accomplish new AFDC goals was to foster constant awareness of the goals and to hold individuals responsible for attaining them.

Working under this new director was very different for the employees at SCDSS. Under Jakes's leadership, according to Summer, there was a "shift of agency focus from child welfare to work." At the same time, Jakes's imposing leadership style created ripples throughout the system. He often evaluated staff's abilities by asking complicated policy questions. Staff who demonstrated good policy knowledge by answering correctly earned his respect.

ALICE SUMMER

Alice Summer had worked for DSS for more than 15 years, first in a county office and then at the state level. She began her professional career with the agency in 1977, following completion of her master's degree in early child education. Summer started at DSS working as a food stamp caseworker in the Richland County office. Over the following 12 years Summer held a variety of positions within the county office including AFDC caseworker, AFDC lead caseworker, AFDC trainer, child protective services case manager, and claims specialist. In 1984, Summer was promoted to unit supervisor, which involved overseeing nine AFDC caseworkers. She continued to work in this role until 1989, when she accepted a position at the state DSS office.

Summer joined the Division of Policy and Planning as a policy writer. Because she had just spent 12 years working directly with DSS clients, Summer came to the state office with numerous ideas for change. She believed that the current DSS service delivery system did not encourage clients ever to achieve the goal of economic self-sufficiency. From her perspective, it appeared that none of the programs were truly geared toward helping a client move his or her family out of poverty. Clients who were successful in finding jobs were not supported throughout the course of their initial employment so that they could develop a sound economic basis for independence. On the contrary, these clients were almost punished for their employment by having their welfare checks quickly reduced and having numerous additional requirements added to their welfare eligibility process. She believed that many aspects of

DSS service delivery could be improved. For example, she thought it would be beneficial to start a pilot program for young mothers. This program could help the women find housing, obtain child care, and train for a job that would eventually allow economic self-sufficiency for them and their children. One of her goals was to help clients realize that they indeed were capable of finding secure employment and supporting themselves. However, as she later reported, she had no idea just how difficult realizing such changes would prove to be.

INITIATING WELFARE REFORM

In February 1995, new welfare reform legislation was introduced in the South Carolina legislature. Numerous Republican politicians had supported it, including Representatives Billy Cotty and John Felder and Senators Larry Martin, Joe Wilson, and David Thomas. When this legislation was first introduced, it represented a new and emerging national trend in attitudes toward public assistance, namely that of assisting recipients in finding employment and becoming economically self-sufficient.

Passed in June 1995, the legislation was termed the Family Independence Act. It promised to bring about many significant changes in South Carolina's welfare policies, two of which were particularly important. The first of these changes was imposing time limits on welfare recipients. More specifically, under the new law, an individual could only receive welfare benefits for 24 months out of any 120-month time period. Furthermore, clients would now be limited to a maximum of 60 months of welfare benefits in a lifetime. The second major change that the Family Independence Act brought about was that every able-bodied adult receiving cash assistance from DSS would now be required to be either employed or enrolled in job training with the goal of eventually obtaining employment. The stated goal of these two changes was to help clients become more self-sufficient, and eventually to gain financial independence.

GAINING COMPLIANCE

This new legislation directly affected the activities of Summer and the rest of the Division of Policy and Planning. Technically, the time limits for welfare clients established under this new South Carolina law were illegal under the federal welfare policies in place at that time. In the past, federal legislators had not supported time limits because they were considered unfair and harmful to welfare recipients. Consequently, in order to enforce time limits, South Carolina would need to obtain a waiver from the federal government.

Jakes approached Summer and other members of her division. "I'd like you folks to write a request for this waiver from the federal policies," he directed.

"You know," Summer responded, "that's going to be a long grueling process, especially because we're one of the first states to ask for permission to impose time limits on welfare recipients."

One of the other members of the division spoke up. "Yeah, we'll have to make a persuasive case for exceptions to federal policy. Then we'll have to wait for the Department of Health and Human Services to spell out the Terms and Conditions, detailing the exceptions that they'll allow us to do."

"Then we'll all have to review the Terms and Conditions and prepare our responses," Summer continued. "This back-and-forth negotiation process will have to continue until all of us are satisfied."

"I know what's involved," Jakes stated matter of factly. "But I really want it done."

Sensing Jakes's insistence, Summer and her coworkers began this lengthy process, which continued for several months. They continued negotiations back and forth with the federal government. Eventually, it seemed that the federal and state policy makers had reached an impasse. The federal government would not agree to grant permission for time limits. However, because time limits represented a core part of Governor Beasley's plan for welfare reform, his office refused to accept the waiver without time limits.

Meanwhile, new legislation was on the horizon for welfare reform at the federal level. Gradually, the national political climate was changing to include an emphasis on welfare reform. In particular, the National Governors' Association played a major role in introducing what came to be known as the Federal Personal Responsibility and Work Opportunity Reconciliation Act during the early months of 1996. One key supporter of this act was Wisconsin governor Tommy Thompson. Interestingly, one aspect of this proposed legislation was time limits for welfare recipients. Based on news reports, Summer and her coworkers recognized that this proposed act would likely pass, and with this realization came a new opportunity for obtaining the waiver.

According to federal policy, if a state had applied for and been granted a waiver before a piece of federal legislation was passed, the state would be permitted to retain any parts of this waiver even if new legislation was passed contrary to the waiver. This meant that if South Carolina accepted the Terms and Conditions that the federal government was proposing before the federal legislation was passed, the state would be allowed to keep all of the provisions in the waiver. Because the new federal proposals included time limits, South Carolina would eventually be granted the right to enact these limits after all. As a result, Summer and other key staff believed that it would be best to accept the federal offer of Terms and Conditions even without the governor's desired time limits.

Summer approached Jakes and explained, "Listen, if we accept the terms and conditions that the feds are offering, even without time limits, then we will get our wavier in and we will have more flexibility when the law passes. It's clear the Personal Responsibility bill is going to pass."

In turn, Jakes presented this idea to Governor Beasley. Jakes was elated when, in July 1996, the governor agreed to accept the Terms and Conditions. One month later, in August 1996, the federal Personal Responsibility and Work Opportunity Reconciliation Act passed as expected. Thus, Summer and DSS staff had not only secured the provisions of their waiver, they could also implement the time limits about which the governor had been so adamant.

IMPLEMENTING WELFARE REFORM

Now that South Carolina had permission to impose time limits on its AFDC recipients, the DSS staff was ready to put the plan into action. However, one major point of contention remained. This area of disagreement centered around the issue of who would be working with the AFDC recipients to enforce the time limits and the requirements for employment or job training.

"I know from my experience in Florida," Jakes insisted, "that these eligibility workers will be too lenient with clients. They won't be able to carry out these tough new reforms."

Jakes also had some firm beliefs regarding the ways in which eligibility workers viewed their clients. "Eligibility workers are bleeding heart social workers; they are incapable of applying any rules that are going to require tough love with clients. They have a very paternalistic relationship with clients and they don't believe in their heart of hearts that these are folks that can actually function, that these are folks that can go out and get a job and do well. They want to say, 'Of course, come on in here and let me give you this $200 a month welfare check because, after all, that's all you can do. You really can't do more than that.'"

"Well, I don't agree with that," Summer responded.

"No," Jakes shook his head emphatically. "They are not going to be willing to apply sanctions, they are not going to be willing to work toward getting people into employment; it's not going to happen. I have had this experience before and it's not going to happen."

"What do you propose instead, then?" Summer asked.

"Using DSS eligibility workers to fill this role was a dismal failure in Florida," Jakes said. "Instead, I want to correct that by hiring a new group of employees from outside of DSS to enact welfare reform legislation. I really think that that's what we should do here in South Carolina."

"How would that work?" Summer asked.

"Well, we keep the current DSS employees, and leave them responsible for determining whether prospective clients would be eligible for financial assistance."

"And the new people?" Summer wondered.

"The new employees," Jakes explained, "would be responsible for working with eligible clients to assist them in finding employment or job training. We could hire them from outside agencies such as the State Labor Office and the Office of Vocational Rehabilitation, where employees actually have experience helping people get jobs. I think we should have both groups in every county office. The 'employment specialists' would help clients get work more quickly, which would enable them to achieve financial independence. You know, that would give clients a better quality of life than depending on public assistance. Of course, it would ultimately diminish taxpayers' expenses, too."

Summer and several of her coworkers had different views. "I doubt that your plan to add another, entirely separate group of workers would be any better at enforcing the new time limits," Summer began. "Plus, where would we find that many new employees?

"Furthermore," Summer continued, "it would be extremely difficult, at best, to locate individuals who would not only have an excellent working knowledge of the business world, but who would also be able to develop effective working relationships with clients."

"What do you mean by that?" Jakes asked.

"Each client and his or her AFDC caseworker need to form a true relationship, and the caseworker should act as an advocate for the client," Summer stated. "This means that the caseworker has to know the exact needs of each of his or her clients. I think that having two separate groups of workers would disrupt these relationships, which would limit the effectiveness of the new program."

"Alright, clarify further," Jakes responded.

"Well, the person who has the greatest influence on a client's beliefs and activities is the DSS worker who is in direct control of his or her welfare money, not some new worker who helps the client find a job. The threat of the new time limits will be stressful enough for clients without them also having to get acquainted with a new DSS caseworker. Besides, hiring this new set of workers is probably going to cause major communication problems between the workers who determine eligibility and those who help find jobs."

"There may be some kinks to work out, but I still believe that we need to hire a new group of workers," Jakes responded. "I know from experience that this will be the best choice."

Jakes's proposal represented a whole new approach for the DSS eligibility workers but Summer and others were not persuaded. Instead of spending more money to hire an additional set of DSS workers, they proposed using these funds to give the current eligibility workers a raise in salary, and lessen their enormous caseloads by hiring more eligibility workers. Therefore, clients would only have to rely on one worker, and this worker would be able to focus better on each client's specific needs.

As time passed, it became more urgent that a decision be made concerning this issue. During spring 1996, Summer and her coworkers stood poised to begin conducting a series of statewide training meetings for the county-level DSS directors. The purpose of these meetings would be to explain the new Family Independence Program and the changes that it would bring to county services. Because of these impending meetings, it was critical that SCDSS staff make a decision about hiring a new group of employees from outside the department. Tensions began to build between Summer and Jakes over their differences of opinion. Based on extensive experience with DSS employees and clients, Summer felt certain that Jakes's plan would not work, and she decided to risk voicing this message to him.

Summer and a coworker believed that their best plan would be to pitch their opinion to Jakes in one last attempt at convincing him to abandon his desire to hire a new group of DSS employees. No final decision had yet been made but they could not proceed without it. Together, they prepared their arguments, and sat down to meet with Jakes.

"You know, the statewide training meetings are going to begin soon," Summer began, well aware of the tense atmosphere in the room. "My colleagues and I are planning to train the directors as if there will be one worker, not two."

Jakes looked skeptical, but did not say anything, so Summer continued.

"I've been working here for 15 years, and I know caseworkers. I believe you're wrong. Trust me on this, our plan is the way to go," she said.

An uncomfortable pause followed. Then Jakes responded, "No, I don't think your plan will work. And besides," he continued, "if I choose to implement your plan, and it fails, as I believe it would, you will be held accountable. It will be on your head."

Summer and her coworker sat for a moment in silence, absorbing what Jakes had just said. It seemed that they had truly reached an impasse. *Where do we go from here*, Summer wondered to herself.

REFERENCE

South Carolina Department of Social
   Services. (n.d.). *DSS program areas*.
   Retrieved October 23, 2002, from
   http://www.state.sc.us/dss/

Case 4

Fran's Questions[1]

VICKI M. RUNNION

F ran quietly closed the door to her office, sat down at her desk, and leaned back in her chair, questions chasing themselves through her mind. *Okay, Frannie,* she asked herself, *What are you going to do?* As strongly as she had come to care about Madeleine and to believe that she might indeed be the best person to work with her, Fran knew that it was appropriate to ask some serious questions.

THE CENTER FOR RECOVERY
AND PERSONAL GROWTH

A small, private, not-for-profit agency with a 20-year history, the Center for Recovery and Personal Growth provided a range of individual and group out-patient services for people with alcohol and drug problems. Typically clients of the center had limited incomes, and many had been cited for driving while intoxicated or similar offenses.

1. Development of this decision case was supported in part by funding from the University of South Carolina College of Social Work. It was prepared solely to provide material for class discussion and not to suggest either effective or ineffective handling of the situation depicted. While based on field research regarding an actual situation, names and certain facts may have been disguised to protect confidentiality. The author and editors wish to thank the anonymous case reporter for her cooperation in making this account available for the benefit of social work students and instructors. Copyright © 2005 Thomson Learning.

Fran Miller had come to work at the center 3 years before in 1991. She brought experience from several prior social work positions, most recently a difficult internship at the Veteran's Hospital working with Vietnam veterans. Although internal problems at the center, such as staff conflict and an atmosphere of disapproval toward the social workers, were frustrating for her, Fran generally felt good about the quality of services the agency provided and enjoyed her work with clients. She had begun a small private practice, working out of her home, about 18 months before, and thought that the different kinds of clients she saw there helped her keep some balance professionally.

AN UNUSUAL CLIENT

Madeleine Greenfeld, 49, had come to the center 6 months before to participate in an educational group for spouses of alcoholics and had continued in the center's codependency counseling group. The director of nursing education at an area hospital, Madeleine was intelligent and articulate, and ready to make changes in her life. Fran had instinctively liked Madeleine, finding her funny and warm. Madeleine's energy level and sense of determination were higher than for many of Fran's clients, and she sometimes found herself surprised when she stood near Madeleine and realized she was only about 5 feet tall and weighed barely a 100 pounds. Similarly surprising to Fran, given Madeleine's professional experience in emergency room nursing and nursing management, was her sometimes timid, childlike response to others' strong expression of emotion.

After the counseling group ended, Madeleine asked if she could see Fran individually for a few sessions, saying that she was concerned about being able to continue identifying and changing problematic patterns in her marriage without Fran's support. At her first individual session, Fran reviewed with Madeleine the significant progress she had made and strategized with her about how to continue with the changes she wanted in her life. Madeleine acknowledged her progress, but said that some other things were coming up that were confusing for her, and that she would like to be able to talk about them with Fran.

"NOTHING LIKE THIS HAS EVER HAPPENED TO ME"

At the next session, something about Madeleine seemed different. Usually one to go right to the point, Madeleine was hesitant and quite soft-spoken when she said, "Fran, something weird is happening. At night when I go to bed I have this sense that someone's face is right beside me. It's like this shadow is there, but I can almost feel someone breathing. I know it's not Jim because he's on his side of the bed. But if he does come close to me, I get really terrified, like I'm frozen and can't move. I'm really scared, Fran. Nothing like this has ever happened to me."

At her next session, Madeleine seemed even more vulnerable, more fragile. More than once, she seemed unable to speak and sat curled up in the chair, her hand over her mouth. After one of the long silences, she almost whispered, "I see a man's face, only I don't know who it is, and bad things are happening, he's doing bad things to me, and I don't know what's going on."

Fran listened intently. Not wanting to distract Madeleine by quizzing her, or to be in any way directive, Fran asked quietly, "Can you see the face?"

Madeleine closed her eyes for a moment, and shook her head, almost imperceptibly. A few moments later she continued, "Something is wrong with me, Fran. I don't understand." After another pause, "I don't know why this is happening."

In another session later that week, while Madeleine was talking, it suddenly seemed to Fran that Madeleine was somehow gone, absent from the room. Her hands in fists, panting, apparently struggling to get up, Madeleine seemed to be terrified, and in pain. Fran was confused at first about what was going on, but she kept her voice very calm, kept talking to Madeleine, calling to her, "Madeleine, it's me—Fran. I'm right here. You're here with me in my office. Nothing is going to hurt you right now."

Madeleine was clearly in agony, and it seemed to last forever. Wondering what was happening, Fran wanted to put her arms around Madeleine and comfort her, but was afraid that any touch might only make things worse. So she just kept talking gently: "Look at me, Madeleine. It's Fran. I'm with you and you're safe. We're in my office. You're going to be okay." For a long while Madeleine made no response.

When Madeleine finally looked directly at her and finally seemed to be present in the office again, Fran was relieved and exhausted. Tentatively, she asked Madeleine, "What did you see? Can you tell me what was happening?"

Her eyes full of confusion, Madeleine shook her head slowly. "I don't know. I see pictures in my head. I don't understand, Fran. I must be making this up—but I don't know why."

SEEKING GUIDANCE

Each session with Madeleine had only raised more questions and intensified Fran's concern for Madeleine, and she lost no time in seeking to better educate herself about various aspects of the case as they emerged. She talked with a couple of colleagues, read some articles they suggested, and began to understand the extent of the professional conflict concerning the issues Madeleine was presenting.

Although she had little trust in her supervisor, Fran realized she had to keep Lori at least minimally informed about some of what was unfolding in her work with Madeleine. Fran dreaded each encounter with Lori, fearing that Lori would insist that she terminate with Madeleine before Fran figured out what was going on, and so she carefully considered what she revealed. But in the passive way Fran had come to expect, Lori approved her requests to continue seeing Madeleine for the present—because, Fran felt sure, Lori had no real clinical insight of her own to offer. More distressing to Fran, she had no confidence that Lori would actually advocate for her, or for Madeleine, if the center's executive director or staff physician suggested termination.

INCREASING TENSIONS

At her next couple of sessions, Madeleine reported having several episodes of panic and terror—at work, on the highway, at home. She acknowledged that once while she was in her car, a part of her wanted to drive really fast and had thoughts about crashing into a wall along the expressway. Fran was immediately concerned about Madeleine's safety, but after exploring these impulses with her, believed that the real risk of suicide was low at present.

Madeleine reported that she was not sleeping well and was fearful that her work would be affected. She described what she referred to as being in "different spaces," and referred frequently to her poor memory. She told Fran about finding herself in the checkout line at the grocery the day before, her cart full of things she hadn't eaten in years. "I didn't remember how to write a check," she said. Then she recounted a trip she had taken over the weekend with her husband. She had gone outside to take a walk, and then later was startled when her husband mentioned that he had enjoyed watching her play basketball all alone on a nearby court. "He said it was like I was a young boy, Fran. What's happening to me?"

With each session, Fran was realizing more of the complexity of Madeleine's story. Even so, the next unfolding jolted her. Madeleine came to a session in the late afternoon, after work. She talked about another example of her "terrible memory." Petite, poised, dressed in a suit that was businesslike and yet feminine, all of a sudden Madeleine leaned forward, knees apart, elbows planted on her knees, a scowl on her face. Fran was just registering how incongruous this behavior was when Madeleine rose, literally stomped over and kicked Fran's chair, and in a voice much rougher than usual, said, "You're just messing everything up!"

Afterward, Madeleine sat shame-faced, unable to speak for some time. Then in a quiet voice, she appealed to Fran, "I am so sorry. Please don't send me away."

From one session to the next, Madeleine's symptoms seemed to intensify, and were more difficult to contain within Fran's office. As Madeleine talked with Fran about her experiences since the last session, she slipped into what Fran came to realize was a flashback. Within minutes, Madeleine shifted from a concerned but calm account of the past week into what seemed an excruciating, all-too-real nightmare, screaming as she relived a torment she could not recall or describe. Once a flashback started, it seemed to Fran that trying to stop it was rather like trying to stop a freight train. She was horrified about what was happening to Madeleine, and at the same time a part of her was aware of how disturbing it must be for her colleagues to hear the screams echoing from her office.

Fran was well aware that Madeleine's emerging issues were taking her far beyond the scope of the center's mission. She started the next session with a gentle confrontation. "I think you're going to need some long-term help, Madeleine. These things that are coming up for you are serious, and this agency isn't the place that can provide the kind of help you need. It's an alcoholism and substance abuse treatment agency, and that's all we do. I can't continue to see you here, but I want to help you find the right person to go through this with you, someone who's really expert in dealing with these issues."

Madeleine's response was immediate: "I know you have a private practice. Will you see me as a private client? Please, Fran. Please help me."

Although the notion of seeing Madeleine as a private client had occurred to her, Fran hesitated. She had to acknowledge to herself that the field of real experts was actually quite small, and that Madeleine's sense of safety with her therapist was crucial to her treatment. She sensed that perhaps she indeed was the one Madeleine could best work with. But she also knew that she was only beginning to understand the magnitude of the challenge she would face.

She wanted to respond in a way that wouldn't push Madeleine away, but also to be sure she wasn't promising more than she could deliver. "I'm not sure, Madeleine. I don't know much about this. I don't know that I have what it will take to help you work through all of it. I think it would be better if you saw someone who knows more than I do. I want to be very clear about that with you. I need some time to think about everything. Can we talk about it at your next session?"

Madeleine sat for a moment. Then, speaking quietly yet forcefully, she said, "This stuff is only starting to come up with you." Standing, Madeleine picked up her bag to leave. But she turned at the door and said, "I won't do this with anyone else, Fran." Her eyes boring into Fran's, she pleaded, "I can't. You're the one."

After Madeleine left, Fran sat unmoving for several minutes. Madeleine's words, "you're the one," reverberated in her mind and she wondered where such a decision would take her.

Although Fran had little hope that a staffing would prove helpful, she felt she needed to consult with administration before deciding to take Madeleine as a private client—not that she wanted to discuss the issue openly with any one of them, but she needed to confirm for herself that there were no better alternatives. She scheduled a special staffing with the center's executive director, the staff physician, and Lori. Fran presented an overview of her work with Madeleine thus far, and summarized what she had learned from reading and from several consultations with experts in cases of this kind.

She had barely begun to discuss her current concerns about Madeleine's ongoing treatment when Theo, the executive director and a former priest, suggested, "Maybe she's possessed. Satan exists, you know. That's what it sounds like to me—evil." Fran knew she needed to keep the disgust and irritation she felt out of her voice as she responded. The last thing she wanted to do was argue with Theo.

But before she could get a word in, Ron, an internist who consulted with the center, responded. "Or more likely, she could be making the whole thing up!" Not bothering to disguise his own disdain for Theo, Ron shifted the focus to his usual area of concern. "This is way outside the center's mission, Fran. You may think that as a social worker you are perfectly well qualified to deal with this woman, but if, just if, there were problems, I doubt that our liability insurance would agree. It's really not appropriate to be addressing these issues here." Fran steeled herself not to react, not to defend herself, or explain the dynamics of the case any further, convinced that Ron was far more concerned about the center's security than about Madeleine's well-being.

Then Lori jumped into the conversation, as usual seeming anxious to align herself with the highest-ranking person present, regardless of previous positions she might have taken. "I concur, Ron, this is not a case we should be seeing here. I haven't really known all that was developing, but now I must insist you close this case as quickly as possible, Fran."

THE QUESTIONS

Fran left the staffing annoyed at yet another example of Lori's self-seeking behavior, but relieved that at least she hadn't been directly advised not to see Madeleine privately. But still she had questions, big ones. Back in her office, she sat at her desk and took a deep breath. *Okay, Frannie,* she asked herself, *What are you going to do?*

The questions came quickly, one after another. *Do I really know enough to work with her competently? Can I learn fast enough to keep up with whatever comes up next? Am I fooling myself just because I like working with her and she trusts me? What about her suicidal thoughts—if it gets worse, can I protect her?*

Some of the questions felt a bit selfish—*Do I really want her coming into my home office? Would it be safe? Do I want my husband, my son—or my neighbors—to hear her screaming?* And Fran felt a bit uncomfortable with these questions. But powerful enough to balance these concerns was one other: *What will happen to her if I don't see her?*

Case 5

Private Charity[1]

MIRIAM McNOWN JOHNSON
KAREN A. GRAY

"This is Bill. Can you come see me in my office?"

"How about in 20 minutes?" Her boss's unexpected call caught Melissa Sinclair by surprise, and she hoped to get through the first draft of a quarterly report before taking a break.

"How about *now*?" Bill insisted.

"Okay."

She walked briskly down the hall and into Executive Director Bill Cannon's corner office. He motioned for her to take a seat across from him at his conference table.

"How are you?" he asked.

"I'm fine," she said, knowing that her health certainly was not what he wanted to talk about.

Lowering his head slightly so he could look over the top of his glasses, Bill peered intently into her eyes. "I need to ask you something. Have you loaned Hao money?"

1. Development of this decision case was supported in part by funding from the University of South Carolina College of Social Work. It was prepared solely to provide material for class discussion and not to suggest either effective or ineffective handling of the situation depicted. While based on field research regarding an actual situation, names and certain facts may have been disguised to protect confidentiality. The author and editors wish to thank the anonymous case reporter for her cooperation in making this account available for the benefit of social work students and instructors. Copyright © 2005 Thomson Learning.

The question caught her off guard. Melissa couldn't gauge what was going on. *Am I in trouble here?* Melissa wondered. Hao Tran worked for her, and she worked for Bill, but for a moment she told herself, *That's none of your business. It was a transaction between friends, outside of our work relationship.* But then she thought, *There's no reason not to tell you.*

"Yes."

"How much?"

"Umm, $500." Melissa searched his face for an expression that might help her guess where this conversation was going.

A FIRST-TIME MANAGEMENT POSITION

Melissa had thoroughly enjoyed almost every aspect of her middle management position over the last three and a half years. She interviewed for the job the same day she defended her master's thesis in December 1979, after a long 5 years of mostly part-time graduate study. She was a little surprised that she got the job. Although she had 10 years of social work experience with her undergraduate degree, all of it was with county DSS agencies. She had only limited experience in actual supervision; she had no experience working with refugees or other international clients of any kind.

It had taken awhile, but Melissa gradually became accustomed to her role as a mid-level manager. At first, when Bill came past her office and announced, "Come on, management team meeting time," she had to remind herself, *Oh yeah,* I'm *a manger now. He's talking to* me.

THE PROGRAMS AND EMPLOYEES

In January 1980, Melissa was hired to be the first director of the URM— Unaccompanied Refugee Minor—Program at Lutheran Social Services (LSS) in Cedar Rapids, Iowa. Through arrangements with the United Nations High Commission on Refugees and the U.S. Department of Naturalization and Immigration, young refugees who had been separated from their parents were arriving from refugee camps in Southeast Asia to be resettled with foster families in the United States. LSS had received a contract from the Iowa Department of Health and Social Services. The contract called for LSS to establish a receiving group home for up to 10 youths who would be assessed and then placed with foster families in four cities across the state.

The majority of their clients would be males in their late teens, mostly Vietnamese or ethnic Chinese from Vietnam, with a handful of Laotians who had fled with other "boat people" to refugee camps in Indonesia. Others had fled overland from Laos to refugee camps in Thailand. Usually their desperate families had made arrangements for the youth to flee the country, knowing that if they were resettled in America, the rest of the family would be given the opportunity for reunification in America at a later time. After a dangerous, often life-threatening escape experience, these young people had lived in the refugee camps for at least several months waiting to be cleared for resettlement. While in the camps they were screened and treated for chronic and contagious health problems, such as hepatitis B or tuberculosis. Once matched and "assured" by a program in the United States, they were flown first to the west coast and then to their final destination. Generally a public welfare agency assumed legal custody while a VolAg (voluntary agency) provided foster care placement and supervision services.

Melissa's first assignment was to hire the group home staff and a Vietnamese interpreter to work with both the group home and the foster families. For the group home she hired a diverse mix of enthusiastic people who had a broad range of experience working with youths. The group home staff amazed her—dealing masterfully with adolescents who were homesick and in culture shock and who rarely spoke more than a few words of English.

In addition to the group home staff, social workers worked with the foster families. Melissa saw these social workers as totally competent and dedicated. She knew that they gave their home phone numbers to all of the foster families and encouraged them to call at any time. She was very excited about the new group home staff, but she felt her best "catch" was the man she hired to interpret, Hao Tran.

Hao was the core of the program. He had a postsecondary degree in pedagogy, had been a classroom teacher in Vietnam, and had come to the United States in the first wave of refugees when Saigon fell in 1975. He was an interpreter with the welfare department in Cedar Rapids and was delighted to leave it for a new job at LSS. He was a man in his 50s, with graying hair that he dyed solid black. He lived with his wife, who earned some money as a seamstress, but didn't speak much English. "She will make you a beautiful *ao dai*,"[2] Hao offered Melissa.

"Doesn't she need a pattern?"

"No, she never needs a pattern. She can measure you and make it. You choose the colors."

Because none of the other staff could speak Vietnamese, and most of the youths were just beginning to learn English, Hao was on call "24/7," for new arrivals, court hearings, registration at school, doctor appointments, transfers to family foster homes, and crises of every kind.

The staff learned that even though most Southeast Asian refugees had experienced significant losses, they were hesitant to discuss their problems

---

2. This is a traditional Vietnamese outfit.

outside of their own families. Melissa had a visual image—the clients she was used to counseling were like small planes with engine trouble, alternately sputtering and gliding to a rough landing. The Southeast Asians were more like a helicopter with a broken blade—they went as far as they could manage on their own and then suddenly dropped like a stone.

Melissa struggled with getting her social work staff to actively recruit and license foster homes when the client arrivals were largely unpredictable, and the program's contact person in the state office was often impatient with both the slow rate of arrivals and the lack of foster homes. But the URM youths trickled in over the next several months, the staff matched youths with foster homes, and the program slowly grew to capacity, more than 40 youths total.

After less than a year with the URM program, Bill asked Melissa to also serve as manager of the resettlement program for refugee families. Volunteers from sponsoring churches did most of the groundwork with the refugee families—locating housing and household goods, arranging clinic appointments, enrolling the younger ones in schools, and matching the older ones with jobs in the community, and getting everyone to ESL (English as a Second Language) classes. There were no volunteers to interpret, though, so the agency employed three bilingual interpreters—Bin Mey, a Cambodian man; Teng Chu, a Hmong man; and Ly Thanh, a Vietnamese woman—who also filled the role of paraprofessional human service workers. There were no Cambodian or Hmong youths in the URM program, but sometimes Teng Chu, who spoke some Laotian, and Ly Thanh could help out with the youths when Hao needed to be elsewhere.

One of the major highlights of the refugee program was the regular ethnic celebrations. Melissa bragged to her friends that she celebrated at least four or five "new years" every year. The celebrations always included fabulous ethnic clothing and music, and potluck dinners with ground beef and noodle casseroles and JELL-O salads (brought by the sponsoring American families) and delicious, exotic, impossible-to-pronounce dishes that the refugees prepared.

After 3 years, the URM program had begun to slowly wind down. With no new arrivals, LSS closed the group home, laid off several staff, and retained others to work as counselors and case managers for the youths moving into independent living situations. Hao continued in his role as interpreter.

MONEY, MONEY, MONEY, MONEY

Hao bought a new home in a nice westside neighborhood and invited everyone to a housewarming. But all was not well. Soon after the housewarming, one of the program staffers confided in Melissa, "I helped Hao understand the closing process, but I really tried to persuade him not to go through with it. He can't afford this house. Other staff told him the same thing, but he won't listen to us. He's caught up in the American dream, I guess."

Then one day Hao asked to see Melissa in her office. In a quiet voice he asked, "Mrs. Sinclair, can I borrow some money until payday?"

"How much do you need?"

"Five hundred dollars, just for 2 weeks, or maybe 3 weeks."

"Let me think about it a minute," Melissa hesitated.

Five hundred dollars was a lot of money, even on a middle manager's salary, but just for a few weeks wasn't asking much. Melissa knew she had to be a bit objective about her decision and that her first consideration must be whether she could afford to lose that much if Hao couldn't pay her back. *I don't give much to charity,* she thought. *This could be my charity project. What good is having money if you can't help worthy people in need?* She was surprised, but not shocked, that Hao was asking her for money. After all, they really trusted each other. She knew Hao would use the money for his mortgage or utilities; he didn't have a gambling or drug problem.

"I'll have to take some funds out of my savings, Hao, but I'll do it. I'd like to ask you why you need it, but I guess it's really not my business."

"Thank you," Hao replied. "I promise I will pay you back."

TROUBLE

It was about 10 days after that, on a Thursday afternoon, when Bill called Melissa into his office. "I need to ask you something. Have you loaned Hao money?"

"Yes."

"How much?"

"Umm, $500."

"What's going on?" Bill asked.

"Hao bought a new house—I think you knew that—and I guess he's gotten in over his head."

Bill shifted his gaze for a moment, then looked her straight in the eyes again. "Did you know he also has borrowed money from four or five other refugee program employees?"

Surprised, Melissa said, "No, no, I didn't know that." Immediately, she thought, *Uh oh. This is trouble. This is more than a loan between two friends.*

"Are you going to do something about it?"

Melissa knew that "No" was not an acceptable response. Melissa respected Bill and his administrative abilities. His background was in business rather than social work, but he had a strong commitment to human services. Melissa liked the way he said he wanted to hear the "bad news" as well as the "good news." His management style was not to rescue employees when things got sticky, but insist that they take care of their responsibilities. He didn't tell people how to do their jobs.

"Yes." Melissa paused, thoughtfully, "I'm not sure just what, but yes, I will."

LIKE A STONE

Friday morning, Melissa caught Hao before he left the office for his first appointment with one of the URM youths. "Hao, I found out you've been borrowing money from a number of people. I'm not concerned about the money I gave you, but I'm concerned that you're in over your head, and you need someone to help you get control of your financial situation. I'd like you to see someone at the Consumer Credit Counseling program at the United Way office. I know the director, Margo Rock. She'll take good care of you. The consumer credit counselor can talk to your creditors and work out payment arrangements that you can manage. Does this sound okay with you?"

Hao nodded silently.

"I don't need to know what you talk about or what you decide to do," Melissa continued. "I just want to know that you're actually attending sessions there."

"Yes, fine, I'll go." Hao appeared docile, with no affect. He seemed neither ashamed nor resistant, but he also did not seem eager to seek out the help.

"Good. I'll call Margo now and tell her I'm sending over a very special person—one of my best employees."

Hao left quickly and quietly.

Melissa felt relieved. *Hao is going to get help, good help. The staff at the Consumer Credit Counseling program are excellent.*

The following Tuesday afternoon, Melissa's secretary buzzed Melissa in her office. "It's Margo Rock. She needs to talk to you right now."

"Hi, Margo. What's up?"

"Your employee, Hao, is here."

"Good."

"No, not good. The counselor said she can't work with him—he's suicidal. She persuaded him to agree to a 'no suicide' contract but only for 24 hours, until he can see you tomorrow. Can I tell him you'll talk to him tomorrow?"

"Sure." Melissa's thoughts raced. "Tell him I'll be in my office all day." Hanging up the phone, Melissa's heart sank. She had hoped the counseling would be a turning point and would get Hao back on track with his finances. *He must be in worse shape than I thought. It sounds like he's coming apart at the seams.*

Melissa thought about how to handle the next day's meeting with Hao. Melissa reflected on what she'd learned in class about suicide. She knew the bottom line game plan was a "no suicide" contract. She hoped that the consumer credit counselor had misread Hao or overreacted; after all, they were financial counselors, not psychotherapists.

Hao appeared at her office door at mid-morning Wednesday.

"Come in."

Hao took a seat across from Melissa's desk.

She looked at him earnestly. "Hao, Margo tells me you're thinking of killing yourself. You know I can't let that happen. Are you really feeling that bad?"

They talked a long time. Melissa tried to get Hao to put his present troubles into perspective. She knew that all refugees had lost a lot: homeland, relatives, career, credentials, culture, and language. They certainly had good reason to be grief stricken. But Hao had come a long way since he left Vietnam. "Look at all you've been through. You lost everything when you had to flee your homeland. You started from scratch here. That must have been really hard but you managed it."

"It was manageable. I was coping," Hao responded. "Except when they killed my son."

Surprised that she had never heard this before, Melissa probed, "They killed your son?"

"The Communist troops took my village and they shot him. Killed him." Without expressing any emotion, Hao's continued. "They left his body in the street. I couldn't leave my house or I would have been shot, too. His body was there in the street for 3 days. Three days. I couldn't do anything."

Melissa pictured a muddy street in a small Vietnamese village and she could feel her eyes tearing up as Hao spoke. But his face showed no emotion. *How can he just sit there like that?* she wondered.

After more conversation, Melissa tried to gauge Hao's risk of suicide. "Do you have a plan about how you would kill yourself?"

"I have a gun, a hunting rifle."

"I don't want you to kill yourself. Can you get rid of it?"

"I have a friend I could give it to. He would keep it for me. I could put it in a box and not even tell him what it is."

"Would you do that, Hao? Would you do that and promise me you won't do anything to hurt yourself without contacting me first?"

"Okay. I'll take it to my friend tonight."

Melissa felt satisfied that she could trust Hao to give the gun away and call her if he was having thoughts of suicide. She had a sense that because he told the credit counselor—a total stranger—that he was suicidal, then maybe he wanted help, and wouldn't hurt or kill himself. Melissa wasn't certain that he wanted to live, but she knew he wasn't going to kill himself that night.

Melissa addressed another matter. "Hao, I can't be your therapist and your supervisor, too. You need to be seeing someone." Melissa knew that Vietnamese people don't like talking to strangers about their personal problems because it brings shame on their families; everything gets dealt with within the family. She also knew that Hao, like most Southeast Asians, tended to defer to authorities and would be reluctant to openly disagree with her. Melissa often thought that the refugee staff she supervised were psychologically incapable of saying the word "no." *Asians want to please, they want things to be harmonious, and they do not like arguments.*

"I'll think about it," Hao said.

This was the best response Melissa knew she could get—she couldn't call to make the appointment because he would need to think it over. She thought he had a better idea than most refugees of the purpose of therapy because he took kids to therapy—actually interpreted in therapy assessments. She had hope that he'd agree to counseling.

Reassured by Hao's responses, Melissa ended the conversation with a request: "Tell me if anything changes."

MORE TROUBLE

Although Melissa believed that Hao was truthful and she was hopeful that he would agree to therapy, her sense of relief was short-lived. Late that day Eva Black, one of the URM foster mothers, called her. Mr. and Mrs. Black had two boys in their home. "We have a crisis here," Mrs. Black confided. "We can't really understand what the boys are saying, but I think. . . ."

Melissa interrupted her. "I think Hao is at the health clinic with another kid, but I can try to track him down for you."

"I'm afraid Hao may be the problem."

"Oh." *Oh no!* Melissa thought to herself, *How can things get any worse?!*

"I think there is money missing from the boys' bank accounts," Mrs. Black continued. "There should be several hundred dollars in each one, and there's almost nothing. Hao opened a joint account for each boy with himself as a cosigner."

"Will you be there for awhile? Let me get right back to you."

Melissa went straight to Bill's office. "We've got a problem. A big problem." She filled him in on her conversation with Mrs. Black.

"What do you plan to do?"

"If Ly Thanh is free tomorrow, I'll ask if she can go with me to talk to the boys and maybe go to the bank. Do you think it's okay to get her involved in this?"

"I don't think you have any other choice," Bill responded. "Keep me posted."

Melissa checked with the other interpreter and called Mrs. Black. "Can you and the boys meet us at the bank tomorrow at 3 P.M.?"

On a hunch, Melissa decided to take a look at the program's petty cash box. The account balanced, but she was surprised to find there were several large IOU's filled out by Hao. It wasn't unusual for staff to put an IOU in if they planned to take a client to lunch or for other small bills, but these weren't client-related expenses and the sums were much larger than a lunch. On the other hand, the fact that he was putting in IOU's was reassuring. He wasn't stealing and was trying to be accountable. But to Melissa it seemed a disturbing indicator of a broader problem.

The visit to the bank the next day confirmed Melissa's worst fears. It was clear that Hao had withdrawn funds from the boys' accounts. Melissa started to feel nauseous. *What about Hao's fragile mental health? If I have to confront him and maybe even fire him, it might push him over the edge. If I don't handle this right, and he kills himself, is his blood on my hands?*

Case 6

One Little Boy (A)[1]

ROBERT JAY PALMER
KAREN A. GRAY

I t was a gorgeous March day, but school social worker Bonnie Cross was indoors doing paperwork when her phone rang.

"Bonnie, this is Marcia. Do you have a minute? I think we have a problem."

"Sure. Go ahead."

"Well, you remember Ben Hartin? This is kind of a long story so bear with me. As you know, Ben's in fifth grade and has been doing fairly well—a little truancy, but overall okay. Today I go in for my weekly visit to Edwards Elementary, and Ms. Hamilton, the principal, tells me about an incident that happened last week. Ben apparently said something disrespectful to Mrs. Scott, his teacher. I don't know what he said, but she told him to go to in-school suspension. He refused to go, so she took the rest of the class to the library while Mr. Almgren, the assistant principal, came in to talk to Ben. Mr. Almgren told Ben he had to go to in-school suspension.

1. Development of this decision case was supported in part by funding from the University of South Carolina College of Social Work. It was prepared solely to provide material for class discussion and not to suggest either effective or ineffective handling of the situation depicted. While based on field research regarding an actual situation, names and certain facts may have been disguised to protect confidentiality. The authors and editors wish to thank the anonymous case reporter for her cooperation in making this account available for the benefit of social work students and instructors. Copyright © 2005 Thomson Learning.

"Then apparently Ben said, 'I won't go with you anywhere. My grand-daddy has a gun at his house in the coat closet and the bullets are in the coffee can in the kitchen. I'm going to get them and kill you and Mrs. Scott and that lady in detention.' I don't know if the fact that Mr. Almgren and the in-school suspension supervisor are African American has anything to do with Ben's response—knowing his family, I wouldn't be surprised. Anyway, they called Ben's dad to come get him.

"Well, Ms. Hamilton freaked out and called the assistant superintendent for administration. She told him about the threat, and that Ben knew exactly where the gun was. He talked to her strictly from the administrative standpoint—that she needed to refer him for expulsion, etc.

"So they wait until I stop by now to tell me this! This happened a week ago! I don't want to get anybody in trouble or anything, but shouldn't they have called the police?"

"Of course they should have!" Bonnie exclaimed. "Oh, god. I think this is an administrative issue now, Marcia, so I'll follow up with the school principal."

"That's fine with me, Bonnie. Thanks for listening and stepping in."

Bonnie hung up the phone and thought, *And after the police, then what?*

ROWAN SALISBURY SCHOOL SYSTEM
AND SOCIAL WORK SERVICES

The Rowan Salisbury School System offices were located in Salisbury, a community of 26,500 in the Piedmont area of North Carolina. Salisbury, the county seat of Rowan County, was 57 percent white and 37 percent African American with 16 percent of the population living below the poverty line. The school system consisted of 17 elementary schools, 7 middle schools, and 6 high schools.

The school district had been employing social workers for 11 years. Starting in 1989, Social Work Services consisted of a coordinator, Bonnie Cross, LCSW, and four full-time LCSWs. Because their duties included internal advocacy for parents, they were district level employees and, therefore, did not report to school principals.

The social workers offered a wide variety of services. Three staff members provided services as school–home liaisons to seven elementary schools and one middle school. These services included home visits, referrals, student and/or parent education groups, peer mediation and conflict management training, and case staffings for special education. One staff member was assigned full time to Early Head Start, where she and family health educators managed the family component. All staff shared the other two middle schools as needs arose. They were also the "crisis response and recovery team" for the school district, and they occasionally developed truancy intervention plans. In addition to serving children and their families, the staff served the district by doing staff development and training for teachers, administrators, and others on topics such as school safety, crisis response, suicide prevention, and dealing effectively with explosive students.

BONNIE CROSS

Bonnie Cross, a native of the Salisbury area, had been the school district's Social Work Services coordinator since the program's inception in 1989. Prior to that position Bonnie was the program director of the Human Services Program at the Rowan County DSS. In addition to the above named duties, Bonnie's responsibilities included serving as a temporary employee assistance program person, the district representative to a variety of community agency task forces and boards, and as a social worker for the alternative school program.

Bonnie was a middle-aged, white woman. She was always impeccably dressed and articulate—she exuded professionalism. She was very productive, and between her other duties, she managed to write several grants per year. Bonnie's accomplishments and demeanor earned her the respect of most of the school district's employees.

MARCIA McNEAL

Marcia McNeal was in her seventh year as a social worker for the Salisbury School District. Marcia received her MSW at age 24 from California State University San Bernardino 9 years earlier, and worked in a day treatment program before moving to North Carolina with her husband and young daughter. During her tenure with the Salisbury School District, Marcia had established a reputation among the district's personnel as being a talented and committed social worker. She, too, was energetic and well respected.

BEN'S HISTORY

After hanging up the phone, and before calling Ms. Hamilton, Bonnie decided to quickly review Ben's records, which began when he was 3 years old. Over the years, Bonnie supervised Marcia regarding Ben's case, so she was familiar with the child, but she wanted a quick refresher. Ben's file was thick, so she quickly flipped through it.

Ben's first referral came in 1992 when a pediatrician referred him for possible developmental delays (see Appendix A). Marcia did an assessment but the family refused preschool services. The next referral came when Ben was in the second grade, and his teacher referred him for behavioral problems (see Appendix B). Ben's parents again declined services, choosing instead to home-school him. Marcia saw Ben next when he was in the third grade (see Appendix C). He was still being homeschooled, but the school district required that Marcia make a home visit. Marcia was concerned that Ben was not actually receiving any educational instruction and the interactions between him and his mother also gave Marcia concern. Once again, Ben's mother declined help. The following year, Ben returned to school for the fourth grade. Ben's principal referred him for repeated absences (see Appendix D). Ben's parents told Marcia about some increasingly serious behavior problems, but still they declined services. At the beginning of Ben's fifth grade year, Marcia checked in with his teacher and found Ben to be adjusting fairly well (see Appendix E). While reviewing Ben's records, Bonnie remembered the details of his history very clearly, and felt ready to proceed.

AFTER MARCIA'S PHONE CALL

Bonnie tried to keep in mind that Ms. Hamilton was in her first year as principal. She had been an assistant principal the previous year and just for one year.

Bonnie called Ms. Hamilton and explained the necessity of calling the police. "When a child makes a threat like that you have to call the police for his, other children's, and your own protection. Remember it's our new policy after Columbine."

"I understand now, and you're right," Ms. Hamilton said, "but I called the assistant superintendent and he didn't tell me to do that."

"I assume he thought you had already done that and you were just looking for the procedural things. Call me back after the police have talked to Ben and his family."

The next day, Ms. Hamilton called Bonnie. "The police said they were quite familiar with Ben because he'd been picked up several times for shoplifting at the mall. They knew where he lived so they went to talk to Ben. They decided not to do anything because Ben said he was just kidding."

Great, Bonnie thought. "Okay. Marcia said you were going for expulsion, so I guess our next step is the expulsion hearing."

THE EXPULSION HEARING

The expulsion hearing, usually held within 3 days of the incident, was postponed for another week to allow Benjamin's mother to attend. But Mrs. Hartin did not attend the hearing after all, though Mr. Hartin did. The school district panel included Dr. Moody (a psychologist from Juvenile Justice), Mr. Almgren,

Mrs. Scott, a school board member, a retired assistant principal, and a retired teacher.

Bonnie could not attend, so the next day she asked Marcia about the hearing.

"Well," Marcia replied, "after Mr. Almgren described the events, Dr. Moody asked if there had been other incidents. Mr. Almgren described some of the other things that have happened since Ben started school. The more questions Dr. Moody asked, the bigger her eyes got. Dr. Moody asked the dad, 'Do you have any control over your son?' He responded, 'No,' with the child sitting right there! Then she said, 'Why do you think the school should be able to control him if *you* can't control him?' Dad said, 'They are trained to do that, I'm not.' Ben sat quietly throughout the entire proceeding. The panel recommended that Ben not be expelled but that he receive a psychiatric evaluation before he returns to school."

"The administration office takes care of those referrals," Bonnie responded, "so there's nothing more for us to do right now."

THE WRONG ASSESSMENT?

A week later, Chrissie Nickels, one of the school psychologists stopped by Bonnie's office. Ms. Nickels was a master level clinician who did psychoeducational assessments to determine eligibility for special education services but not counseling.

"Hi, Bonnie. Ben Hartin was referred to me for a psychological evaluation. Could you give me some background on him?"

"Ben was referred for a psychiatric eval," Bonnie responded, "not a psychological."

"Well, here's the letter the superintendent wrote the parents. It says Ben's been referred for a psychological assessment to be done by a psychologist in his school district."

"That won't do! That child needs a psychiatric evaluation! We need a psychiatric evaluation! We really would have liked to have one the day he made these threats. If we'd been called that day, we'd have followed our department policy that says if we think a child is suicidal or homicidal, we require that the parents come pick the child up and take them to a qualified mental health professional to be evaluated. We want an outside professional opinion. I'm sorry, Chrissie, but can you hold off?"

"Sure," Ms. Nickels replied. "I'll wait to hear from you," and she left.

Bonnie was fed up. *This kid's been slipping through the cracks for years. Two weeks ago, he threatened to kill somebody and* nothing's been done! *He's a ticking time bomb and we're just plodding along like he's some kid who's not dangerous. We could very well be the next Columbine. What do I need to do to wake administration up?!*

Appendix A

Rowan Salisbury School System
Intake Form

Intake Date: _10/14/92_

Client Name: _Benjamin Hartin_   Race: _White_

Social Security: _555-55-5555_   DOB: _March 10, 1989_

Parent/Guardian Name: _Don Hartin_

Parent/Guardian Name: _Dorothy Hartin_

Sibling(s) Name and Age: _None_

Sibling(s) Name and Age: _____

Address: _1111 Pineview Rd, Piedmont, NC 28144_   Phone: _704-111-1111_

Reason for Referral:

Benjamin Hartin was referred to this office by our consultation team's developmental pediatrician, Dr. Joseph. Dr. Joseph feels that Ben should be in preschool because he might be developmentally delayed.

At 9:30 A.M. on 10/14/92, I arrived at the Hartin home to complete my intake assessment. Dorothy reported that she took Benjamin to the doctor, as he was overly "fussy." She reported that the doctor told her that he might be developmentally delayed. Dorothy was not sure what that meant and assumed it explained his behavioral problems.

Developmental History:

Dorothy said that her pregnancy with Ben was difficult and that he was a "difficult baby." Dorothy did not know when Benjamin began eating solid food. He began to crawl at 9 months, walk at 20 months, and was toilet trained around age 3. Benjamin's first words were "no" and "ma" at 13 months.

Health:

Benjamin has had no major heath problems and no allergies.

Family History:

Dorothy and Don Hartin married in 1988, after dating 2 years, when they found out Dorothy was pregnant. Both grew up in Salisbury and received their high school diplomas from the same high school. Neither Mr. nor Mrs. Hartin report that they were ever in LD classrooms as a child. Neither partner has any previous marriages or children. Dorothy reported that Benjamin was her first and only pregnancy. Dorothy's parents live in Salisbury and she has one brother who is in the military. Don's parents also live in Salisbury and he is an only child. Dorothy reported that her parents drink daily but there have been no mental/ physical health problems in her family of origin. Don reported that there are no substance abuse problems in his family but his mother's cousin has a cognitive disability.

Behavioral Concerns:
Dorothy and Don report that Benjamin "does not listen." He throws things when he is mad or wants attention. They also report that he cries a lot.

Assessment:
When I arrived, the Hartins invited me into their living room. The house is located in a working-class neighborhood and the house was clean. Don was dressed in jeans and a t-shirt, Dorothy in a housecoat. Don had a full, untrimmed beard and his hair was not combed. Benjamin was in the kitchen, peeking around the corner. As I began to introduce myself to Benjamin's parents, Ben began throwing things at me from the kitchen—toys, books, and whatever he seemed to find. Neither parent acknowledged that anything unusual was happening. After several minutes of this behavior, I finally told Benjamin that he had to stop. At that point, Benjamin slowly crept into the room.

After a few minutes of describing the program to the Hartin's, Ben retired quietly back into the kitchen and played with pots and pans. I continued the intake session and learned that Dorothy was 33 and Don was 34, although Don looks older. Dorothy stays home and cares for Benjamin and Don works at the airport in Charlotte. This was their first marriage and neither had any other children. Dorothy reported she had a difficult pregnancy and that Benjamin was a difficult baby as he cried a lot. Dorothy then sighed and stated, "he still is difficult." Although they have some family around, Dorothy reported that they have had very little help. Don interjected that there was no help from Dorothy's family, as her parents were known to "tide one over." He then commented that they would not need help if Dorothy would let him "take out the switch."

Don asked for help reading the forms. In addition, I explained the program several different times to make sure that he understood. After that, both parents seemed to understand the program and indicated that they were both interested in getting Ben into preschool.

Next scheduled appointed 10/21/92 at 10:30 A.M. to complete preschool paperwork.

Social worker's opinion: Parents signed a medical release form so that I can review Ben's records. Ben has some unusual physical features, and I want to see if there was a genetic consult.

Client Name: Benjamin Hartin **SS#:** 555-55-5555 **DOB:** March 10, 1989	
Date	**Progress Notes**
10/21/92	The Hartins did not show for office appointment. I called and spoke to Dorothy. She reported that they had forgotten. The appointment was rescheduled for 10/25/92.
10/25/92	The Hartins did not show for office appointment. The appointment was rescheduled for 10/31/92.
10/31/92	The Hartins did not show for office appointment. When staff spoke with Dorothy, Dorothy reported that it is too difficult to get out. Dorothy agreed to a home visit on 11/8/92.
11/8/92	I arrived at the Hartin's home at 4:30 P.M. and found the family in the front yard. Dorothy was sitting in a chair while Don was fixing the screen door. Dorothy pulled up a chair for me to sit down. I did so just as Benjamin picked up a kitten. He was pulling the kittens legs apart until the kitten was screaming. The parents did not intervene so I instructed Ben to put the kitten down, that he was hurting the kitten. He did so. I attempted to talk to his parents about the incident when Don interrupted me and asked me to leave, as they were about to leave. They refused to set another appointment, instead asking me to call them later.
11/15/92	Spoke with Dorothy on the phone. She stated that they have decided not to send Benjamin to preschool and would not need school services at this time, saying, "We can handle Ben ourselves."

Appendix B

Client Name: <u>Benjamin Hartin</u> SS#: <u>555-55-5555</u> DOB: <u>March 10, 1989</u>	
Date	**Progress Notes**
11/12/96	Lucia Mathews, Benjamin's second grade school teacher, referred Benjamin Hartin to this office. Refused to do work. Refused to come to school. Parents asked for testing. Due to classroom behavioral problems, she requested that a psychoeducational test be completed on Benjamin.
	Per Ms. Mathews, Ben's mother and father separated for a while and Ben lived with his mother in another school district. He never did attend preschool but attended kindergarten there. The parents got back together and Ben began in our school district in the first grade. Per Ms. Mathews, other than having a tendency to isolate himself from other children, it seems he did pretty well. He is currently in Ms. Mathews' second grade class. Ms. Mathews reported that she has been having difficulty getting Benjamin to do his work at school and he has missed several days. He had some extreme behavioral disruptions and was having difficulty completing assignments. She thought he should get some psychoeducational testing to see what's going on with him, so she went through all of the necessary documentation and referral procedures.
	On 11/12/96, I arrived at the Hartin residence. Dorothy met me at the door and invited me in. She reported that Don was at work and that Benjamin was in bed sick. Dorothy reported that Benjamin yells at her and refuses to listen. Dorothy agreed to have the psychoeducational test completed on Benjamin. She signed the paperwork. At the end of the session, Benjamin came out of his bedroom and sat on the couch. When I spoke to him, Benjamin did not answer.
12/4/96	Dorothy and Benjamin Hartin met with Dr. Moody [the school psychologist] and me to discuss testing scheduled for tomorrow, 12/5/1996.
12/5/96	Received a phone call from Benjamin's mother. She stated that she was concerned that if Ben is tested as being "handicapped" he would be placed in special education classes and that she did not want that to happen. Consequently, she is canceling the testing appointment. I explained that the purpose of the tests was to assist Ben in getting the supports he needs to get the best education possible, but was unable to dissuade her from canceling the appointment. Ben's mother then said, "I'm tired of trying to get Ben to go to school and I'm tired of the attendance people calling me all the time, so I'm going to school him at home."
	We discussed the pros and cons of this idea, including whether Dorothy would be as capable as a teacher, whether Ben would get as good an education, etc. Dorothy still feels that homeschooling is best. I referred her to the homeschooling association.

Appendix C

Client Name: _Benjamin Hartin_ **SS#:** _555-55-5555_ **DOB:** _March 10, 1989_	
Date	**Progress Notes**
11/13/97	Ben is still being homeschooled. Because his mother is not part of the home-school association and because he is being homeschooled under the auspices of the school district, I was required to make a home visit. I arrived at Ben's home and Dorothy invited me in. She apologized for her appearance; she said she hadn't been sleeping much and was exhausted. We sat down and she quickly told me that Ben's dad left at the beginning of the school year. Ben has been living with her, but he spends a lot of time with his dad and dad's parents. According to Dorothy, Don's parents aren't able to supervise him because of their frail health, and Don doesn't intervene much either. Dorothy stated she was very flustered and frustrated with Ben because he won't listen or do what he's told. When I asked her about homeschooling, she quickly stated that she was teaching him. At that point, Benjamin came into the room and sat down on the couch and told his mother to get him some milk. Dorothy immediately jumped up to get him some milk. I asked Benjamin how he was and he said he was "fine." Then he got up, kicked the door and yelled at his mom to get the milk faster. Discussed again with Dorothy whether homeschooling is the best option for Ben. She maintains that it is. She is not interested in the homeschooling association.

Appendix D

Client Name: _Benjamin Hartin_	SS#: _555-55-5555_	DOB: _March 10, 1989_

Date	Progress Notes
12/01/98	Received a referral from Ben's principal because of repeated absences from school. I first spoke with Ben's teacher. She said Ben is back in school this year because Mom couldn't handle him at home. Mom wanted to complete the testing and this time Ben was tested. He tested as having a significant discrepancy between his ability and achievement, which qualified him as learning disabled (LD). The school psychologist thought that Ben's poor test scores may have been a result of his being "homeschooled" last year. Ben was placed in an LD course for one period each day. Ben did really well there and so they placed him back into regular classes in October. His behavior and academics seem to be fine; the primary concern is perpetual absences from school. Truancy officer spoke with both dad and grandparents. Ben moves back and forth quite a bit, spending the night at either home. Several times the officer helped parents get Ben out of bed and to school. On other occasions, he wasn't at home or at school, and so the officer drove around until he found Ben who claimed he was going to the mall.
12/03/98	Made a home visit. Ben's parents are living together in a house across the street from Don Hartin's parents. Dorothy said that while Ben was staying with his grandparents he set fire to his grandfather's bed because he was angry with the grandfather over something grandfather asked him to do. Ben set the fire under the bed, then went outside with grandparents. Twenty minutes later Ben told grandparents that they might want to check the bedroom. The fire department put out the fire. (There is no history of sexual abuse. However, see previous records re: pet abuse.) Dorothy not interested in mental health services. During conversation with Don about what he does when Ben disobeys, Don shared that when Ben was little, he had attempted to discipline him and DSS came out. Ben was 3 or 4. Don said he just "washed my hands of it. I can't do anything because it's too much." Don and I discussed other means of discipline and ways to manage Ben. Helped Dorothy make a plan to get Ben to school and on time. Dorothy quite agreeable.
12/04/98	Social worker's opinion: I am concerned about parents' ability to comprehend the seriousness of Ben's actions, and their ability to follow through with the help he needs. They seem to be overwhelmed. Relayed above information to Ben's principal. He will call me if there are further truancy problems.

Appendix E

Client Name: Benjamin Hartin   SS#: 555-55-5555   DOB: March 10, 1989
Date   **Progress Notes**

Date	Progress Notes
9/15/99	Checked in with Ben's teacher, Mrs. Scott, to see how the year was going so far. She said things were going well. Because of Ben's history and the possibility of his previous behavior recurring, I offered her some advice. I suggested that she "catch" Ben doing something good and reward him with positive behavior, but don't say, "that's so great!" I told her to say, "I see you've finished your work. Would you like a pencil or a sticker?" If they want praise, they'll ask for it, e.g., "aren't you proud of me?" Otherwise, they see praise as false praise. The best way to handle him is to give him choices. Also, if you need to pull him out of the room, the best thing to do is to have all the other kids leave the room. I gave her a handout that Bonnie made about this.
11/30/99	I checked in briefly with Ben on the playground. He was not playing with any other children. I asked him if he was still living with his Mom and Dad, and he said his Mom moved out. He told me he hates his Mom. He said his likes his teacher. Checked in with Ben's teacher. Although there are still problems with truancy, most of the time Ben comes to school and does his work.

Case 7

In Good Faith[1]

F. MATTHEW SCHOBERT, JR.

"Louis is unaccounted for," executive director Pete Langen announced in his characteristically laconic New England manner, typical of his ability to say a mouthful with just a few words. It was the April 2001 meeting of Food for All's board of directors and Pete's comment, brief though it was, immediately captured everyone's attention.

"What do you mean, 'unaccounted for'?" Brenda Rivas asked. A note of caution echoed in her voice.

"Unaccounted for," shrugged Pete, apparently unsure of what else to say. "He hasn't returned to Jacmel but he's not at CIRAD. I spoke with Blaise a couple days ago and asked about Louis. Blaise said Louis never returned home. So I called CIRAD to see if he was still there doing additional training, but they said he was not there and had never even arrived."

A disturbing quiet settled over the group. Pete finally uttered what everyone feared, "It doesn't look like Louis is going back to Haiti."

After an uncomfortable pause, Allison Crane broke the silence. "Well, aren't we going to report this to INS?" Her tone of voice was clear; she was charting

1. Development of this decision case was supported in part by funding from the North American Association of Christians in Social Work. It was prepared solely to provide material for class discussion and not to suggest either effective or ineffective handling of the situation depicted. While based on field research regarding an actual situation, names and certain facts may have been disguised to protect confidentiality. The author and editors wish to thank the anonymous case reporter for his cooperation in making this account available for the benefit of social work students and instructors. Revised from Schobert, M. (2003). In good faith. *Social Work & Christianity, 30*(2), 178–188. Copyright © 2003 NACSW.

a course of action, rather than voicing a question for discussion. Brandon Dicorte's level of unease skyrocketed.

FOOD FOR ALL

Located in central Louisiana, just north of Alexandria, Food for All (FFA) was a faith-based, nonprofit organization of Christian volunteers and professionals committed to the alleviation of global hunger. It was started in 1974 by an ecumenical partnership of agricultural missionaries from the Mennonite Central Committee (MCC) and the United Methodist Committee on Relief (UMCOR). FFA worked toward its mission by providing training, education, and on-site assistance in sustainable agricultural development, appropriate technologies for resource-poor communities in developing countries, and conservation. The bulk of FFA's funding came from individual donors, churches, and local foundations, but FFA also operated a number of income-generating projects, such as a community supported organic garden and a fair-trade store that offered coffees, teas, and a wide variety of handmade goods from artisans in developing countries. FFA conducted community education, awareness, and outreach programs for the local and regional community. The centerpiece of their work, however, was training interns who would practice and teach sustainable agriculture in rural international settings.

FFA recruited domestic and international candidates for 15- and 12-month internships, respectively. FFA was not a sending agency; it did not sponsor, commission, or financially support international development workers. Domestic interns, therefore, typically came to FFA from Christian or humanitarian mission or relief and development agencies, often through connections with MCC or UMCOR, for 15 months of training and education. Domestic interns spent 9 months at Food for All, followed by 3 months at an on-site FFA agricultural development partnership program at one of four locations in Central America. Interns completed their training with a 3-month capstone experience back at FFA where they integrated their work in Central America with their training at FFA. They also reflected on and shared their on-site agricultural experiences with others at FFA and with local community organizations.

International interns came from countries around the world, particularly tropical countries in Central America, Sub-Saharan Africa, and South-Central Asia for a 12-month internship program. These interns went through the same application process as domestic interns. They completed a lengthy application packet that required detailed personal information, educational background, professional skills, work experience, and a list of references. Applicants also had to write brief responses to six essay questions and an additional essay describing why they wanted to intern at FFA, what they hoped to learn, and how they planned on using what they learned after completing the internship. In addition, international interns were required to secure an H-3 visa to enter the

United States. H–3 visas permitted international interns to enter the United States temporarily to receive education and training. These visas lasted the duration of a training program, but could not exceed 2 years. FFA assisted international applicants with the application process and the agency paid all fees and expenses for an H-3 12-month business-training visa. At the end of the 12-month period, international interns returned to their home countries and introduced the training and education they learned from FFA to their local communities.

International interns made several unique contributions to FFA's mission. Primarily, these interns "internationalized" FFA. They provided unique opportunities for FFA staff, volunteers, supporters, and especially domestic interns to interact with and learn from people of other cultures. This process began preparing domestic interns for cross-cultural experiences and challenges they would face when they traveled to their host country. International interns also represented, to FFA supporters and to local and regional communities, the driving purpose of the organization—to work toward the alleviation of hunger in developing countries. These interns also made unparalleled contributions to FFA's work because they generally represented key leaders and decision makers in their communities of origin. International interns were embedded in the history, culture, and values of their communities and countries. They possessed keen awareness of their communities' strengths and weaknesses, of local assets and needs, and could often identify what agricultural practices and technological interventions would or would not work in those contexts. Plus, international interns shared their knowledge of agricultural methodology, practice, and skills with FFA staff and domestic interns, enriching and expanding the agency's knowledge base and skill set.

Perhaps the single most important aspect of hosting international interns was that, on returning to their homes, they were naturally viewed as "one of the community." They were indigenous, insiders rather than outsiders. This bypassed myriad cross-cultural and relationship-building obstacles common in international relief and development work. Additionally, because international interns were returning home, their level of investment and commitment usually far exceeded that of domestic interns whose work, while crucial, often lasted for only a matter of months or years, as opposed to decades and generations. In their efforts to alleviate global hunger and reduce poverty, FFA staff and supporters understood that international interns represented the most effective and efficient use of the agency's limited resources.

BRANDON DICORTE, LMSW

Although Brandon Dicorte was the newest FFA staff member, he had a long history with the organization. Brandon had attended Louisiana College, a small, liberal arts, Christian university located outside of Alexandria. Brandon majored in social work and public administration. During his years as an undergraduate, he volunteered at FFA through community service programs at Louisiana College and with members of Hope Chapel, a small, nondenominational congregation he attended. After college Brandon enrolled in a graduate social work program at Tulane University in New Orleans. He earned his master's degree in social work with a concentration in health care and started working in pediatric oncology at Tulane University Hospital and Clinic. Three years later he returned to Alexandria when Laura, his wife, began her medical residency program at Community Family Practice, a holistic health care clinic that served low-income and uninsured people and families. Shortly after this move, Brandon was hired as a social work supervisor at St. Mary's Children's Home. For the next 10 years he worked at St. Mary's.

Brandon and Laura joined Reconcilers Fellowship, a bilingual, multicultural Mennonite church. About 60 people attended this small house church. It was completely lay led; there were no paid staff. Pastoral responsibilities rotated between three men, and men and women shared equally in all teaching responsibilities. The community worshiped in English and Spanish, although not everyone was bilingual. Another distinctive mark of this small congregation was its high level of commitment to social ministries. Nearly every member of Reconcilers Fellowship was actively involved in Christian service. Some worked with Habitat for Humanity, others volunteered in after-school tutoring programs for children, several worked at local food banks and homeless shelters, and all of them advocated for peace and nonviolence. Many members of this congregation were also active supporters of FFA. This community's sense of compassion and justice for the poor and vulnerable struck a chord with the Dicortes. These Christians with whom Brandon and Laura worshiped and formed a community took the radical nature of Christian discipleship very seriously. Their commitment to living the ethics of the kingdom of God, as Jesus taught in the Sermon on the Mount (Matthew 5–7; cf. Luke 6:17–49), challenged and nurtured Brandon to live a life shaped by the Gospel, rather than to settle for a comfortable form of cultural Christianity. Christian ethics also sustained his commitment to social work practice.

With the birth of their second child, Brandon began considering other employment options. He no longer wanted to be on call 24-hours a day several days a week, as he now was as one of the senior social work administrators for St. Mary's. Brandon wanted more time with his sons and he desperately wanted to work more directly on issues of social justice. Learning of these desires, Pete and several members of FFA's board, some of whom attended Reconcilers Fellowship, approached Brandon about the possibility of assuming some of the agency's administrative, business, and development work in order to free Pete to focus more on training interns and managing operations of the 60-acre farm. Recruiting Brandon, because of his administrative experience at St. Mary's, reflected FFA's organizational growth toward building a more specialized staff. This seemed just the opportunity Brandon had prayed for. He could reduce his workload, spend more time with his wife and children, and work with what he considered to be a unique faith-based organization. Brandon joined the staff in November 2000 as their first development director. Five months later he found himself in a most uncomfortable predicament.

LOUIS TOUISSANT

Louis Touissant was a rather large man; he was stocky and nearly 6 feet tall. His imposing size belied a quiet, gracious, extremely deferential personality. Perhaps his personality had been tempered by the 40-odd years of grinding poverty and inescapable suffering he knew from rural village life in Haiti; perhaps it reflected a combination of cultural deference and his limited English language skills.

Louis arrived at FFA in June 2000, several months before Brandon joined the staff. Louis, like Brandon, was no stranger to FFA. FFA had worked in the rugged rural landscape of southeastern Haiti, particularly in the village of Petit Jacmel, since 1981. Louis participated in FFA's development work in Jacmel from the very beginning. In 1987, his older brother, Blaise, successfully founded Food for Haiti (FFH), a sister-agency to FFA. FFA and FFH worked closely together to promote agricultural, technical, and educational programs in the village and district of Jacmel. Louis, who had completed agroforestry training at Port-au-Prince's Agricultural Polytechnic Institute, taught basic agroforestry skills and education at FFH's training center. He often expressed an interest in coming to FFA for additional training and education. Because his English skills were far too limited to make him an eligible intern candidate, he enrolled in several English courses in Jacmel. Louis earned high marks in every class and finally achieved his goal—he applied to FFA and was accepted as an intern.

Unfortunately, Louis did not adjust well to life in central Louisiana or as a FFA intern. Being from the tropics, he had great difficulty coping with the cool fall and cold winter weather. And, despite the good grades he earned in his English courses, his language skills proved to be much poorer than anyone expected. As a result, he had a hard time communicating and understanding.

Louis's relationship with the staff and other interns soon became strained when he refused to share in domestic chores that were part of life on the farm and in the dormitory. Although these communal responsibilities had been explained in the application materials, Louis seemed to think that men, particularly educated men like himself, did not participate in preparing or cleaning up after meals, doing dishes, or general cleaning in the dining hall, kitchens, and bathrooms. These tasks belonged to women and children. His attitudes about gender did not entirely surprise the staff at FFA. They had experienced this reaction from other men from developing countries. But, it did create added tensions between Louis and some of the interns, particularly with female interns who Louis expected to do his dormitory chores for him.

Something else, however, did surprise FFA's staff. Louis began talking about going to Christian International Relief and Development (CIRAD), another agricultural development agency, located in Sarasota, Florida, for additional training and education. Louis broached this topic with Pete on several occasions. Brandon, whose office was across the hall from Pete's, often overheard these conversations. On a particularly cold day in February, Louis announced he was going to CIRAD and from CIRAD he would return to Petit Jacmel. Pete and Brandon tried, but failed, to convince Louis to finish his internship at FFA. Before Louis departed, Pete and Brandon made it a point to discuss Louis's visa restrictions with him, emphasizing his responsibility to adhere to his August return date. Louis had spent nearly 8 months improving his English and they were painfully clear with him on this point. Louis reassured them he would return to Haiti in accordance with his visa.

Once Louis left FFA, Pete and Brandon never heard from him again. Louis never contacted them. He never arrived at CIRAD. He never contacted his brother. He never returned to Haiti.

THE BOARD MEETING

FFA enjoyed strong support from a deeply committed and very active board of directors. The board made decisions and set policy for the agency, and nearly every member was involved with at least one of FFA's projects. Most were well known to the interns and volunteers. The board met every other month and standing committees met between board meetings. FFA's standing committees included Executive, Program, Fundraising and Development, and Public Relations. Pete served as the ex officio member of the Executive and Program committees and Brandon was the ex officio member on the Fundraising and Development and the Public Relations committees. Although Pete and Brandon were not members of the board, they worked very closely with these committees, submitted staff reports, and were involved, to a large degree, in the agency's decision-making processes.

Everyone at FFA was active in Christian congregations. Ironically, despite their deep faith commitments, neither the board nor the staff engaged in much "religious" or "God" talk. They shared a common worldview that informed FFA's mission and were committed to working for and alongside the world's poor. Theologically, everyone enjoyed a strong kinship.

Pete, Brandon, and two of the board members worshiped together at Reconcilers Fellowship, three others attended mainline Protestant churches, and the remaining two attended a large interdenominational, urban church known for its service to the urban poor. This contributed significantly to the deep theological and vocational connections shared between staff and board members. Everyone knew one another well enough that the obvious—their commitment to following Christ and the practical implications and application of that commitment—was implicitly a part of their conversations. It rarely needed to be made explicit.

Yet, in spite of all of this, Pete's disclosure to the board that Louis had disappeared elicited a wide range of strong reactions from board members. "Well, aren't we going to report this to INS?" was one of the first remarks. When Brandon heard it, he became tense and nervous. He foresaw a serious fight brewing.

"I don't think that's appropriate," Pete replied. "It was Louis's responsibility to leave the country, not ours to make sure he left. Even though our name is on the visa, INS does not give us that responsibility. They never say anything like that in any of the paperwork."

"Well, what have we done in the past?" Allen Jeffreys asked. "Has this happened before?" Allen had joined the board the previous year and, although he was still rather new, he had a knack for seeing multiple solutions to vexing problems. This had proven helpful in resolving tough decisions in the past.

Pete and Angela Santos, the board president, exchanged looks, and, after a thoughtful pause, each shook their heads. "No," they both replied in unison.

"This is the first instance in, what, the 20-something years we've worked with international interns," Angela continued. "I don't believe we have any written policies on this either." Pete's body language indicated she was correct.

"Do you think this will affect future opportunities for getting visas for other applicants, I mean, if INS or someone finds out?" Brenda asked.

Brandon noticed that Allison nodded in agreement. Brenda and Allison were often quick to consider legal and liability issues that might affect the agency.

"I for one think we need a policy to protect ourselves," Jesse Farrar chimed in. Jesse was not on the board of directors yet, but his wife, Elizabeth, was and it was a board tradition to invite potential board members to a meeting before issuing them an invitation to join the board. "I don't want this agency to look like a wormhole for illegal immigration. I mean, he basically used us to immigrate, didn't he? Isn't that about right? We can't be seen as somehow encouraging this or as being an easy way for people to come into the country. Do we want to be seen as, 'If you want an easy way into America, try this'?"

"I think it's really easy for people to think that way, Jesse," Brandon intervened. "There's an element of anger we're all feeling over this because that's not why we're here. We're not getting money from donors to run a nonprofit organization that trains international interns in sustainable agriculture and then to have them remain here and not return home. I understand some of us being quite upset and wanting to act on that. I just don't know how productive it will be."

"But somehow," Allison stressed, "we've got to write into policy that we will report them if they don't return home. We need to be stronger on this than we are. And if not a policy," she blurted out in near exasperation, "then what?"

"What about our intern screening process?" Allen suggested. "Is there a problem with it? I mean, are there weaknesses in how we recruit and screen potential interns? If some of us are uncomfortable with creating new policies, then perhaps we should consider other things we could do to safeguard ourselves and ensure that international interns do return home—willingly."

"Hey, the screening process can't be that flawed," Percy Manning observed. "I mean, 20-something years—isn't that what you said, Angela?—and this is the first time this has happened. Maybe this was the exception."

"Or, perhaps we made an error in judging Louis's application," Pete mumbled.

"What do you mean?" A couple of people spoke at once.

"We've been successful in not having any international interns go AWOL," Pete began, with a rather dejected sigh, "not because we've been lucky, but because we've always determined that they have sufficient family connections back home to make it as unlikely as possible they would consider staying in the States. Until Louis, this meant that we've only accepted married men, usually fathers, as interns. We've resisted pressure to accept spouses or children because, with their family present, that would make it all the easier for them to decide to stay here and violate their visa."

"And Louis, although he is Blaise's brother and has other brothers and sisters in Jacmel," Angela finished Pete's thought, "was single and had no children."

"Why did we accept him, then?" Jesse asked.

"We thought we knew him well enough. We've known him since we started working in Jacmel, when he was a young man. I saw Louis more as a partner in our work in Haiti than as an international intern. It seemed like a great opportunity for all of us," answered Pete.

"I just can't believe Louis did this!" Elizabeth moaned.

"It's frustrating, I know," Brandon replied, "to face this lost opportunity, but Louis's decision isn't too hard to understand. There are tens of thousands of Haitians living in south Florida; he even has friends from Jacmel living there. It's entirely possible to understand some of what he was thinking and why he did what he did."

"It's completely understandable," Pete said, a bit more energetically. "He got introduced to American culture. He can find a minimum wage job here and make far more than he ever could back in Haiti and he can get involved in Florida's Haitian community. It's all completely rational, what's irrational is going back! So, frankly, I'm rather sympathetic and just don't see any reason we should sic our government on him. I mean, most of us don't even believe immigration should be illegal or restricted from poor, developing countries like Haiti. It boils down to an issue of justice, if you ask me. So, it just doesn't follow that since we're in business because we're called to be compassionate to those who suffer, to help them realize opportunities and create better futures for them and their families and their communities—for people like Louis— that we should be a part of forcing them back into lives of poverty and despair.

How can we turn around and, just because Louis chose not to go back to Haiti, start calling the government to hunt this guy down and deport him?"

"I agree," interjected Catherine Kendrick. Catherine was a member of a lay Franciscan order. She had long worked with Christian organizations, both in the United States and internationally, on many social justice issues, particularly poverty, hunger, peace and nonviolence, and racial reconciliation. She joined the board the previous year, and was already well respected in the organization. "We're supposed to be people of compassion," she continued. "We are called, over and over again in scripture, to care for the stranger in our land. I mean it's all over the place. And I don't think we can rationalize having Louis prosecuted for immigrating here and think we are doing what God would have us do. What Louis did may be 'illegal,' but in matters of faith, I think we owe a greater responsibility to honoring God and loving our neighbor."

"Sure, I hear what you're saying, Catherine, but I'm concerned about our liability," Allison replied. "Aren't we liable to the INS? Can't they fine us or get us into trouble? Plus, won't this hurt our chances for getting other interns? And what if word gets out in the community? Do you think people will think twice about supporting us financially if they think we're looking the other way on issues like this? I think we need to be very proactive about preventing this from happening again."

"But Allison, there's nothing in their literature about us being responsible for this. It rests solely with the INS," Pete reiterated.

"So, what you're saying is that we're not *legally* responsible for this in any way?" Percy asked. "Alright, I can live with that, and quite honestly I'm with Catherine on this one, but, perhaps we should consider what we as an agency should do. You know, what is the ethical thing for us to do?"

"Percy has a point," Brandon interjected, "it seems like we need to move from 'We don't have to do anything' to considering, 'What, in good faith, should we do?' "

"Good point, Brandon," Angela remarked. "What do *you* think we should do?"

Case 8

Planet Methadone[1]

VICKI M. RUNNION

Transitions, the methadone clinic where Kerry Carson worked, was closing—for the day. Kerry began packing his backpack, eager to head for home—anywhere away from Transitions—where he could sit and think. Getting on his bike and doing something physical would be a relief from the strain of this afternoon. *Getting stuck between Dr. Arthur and Ella could get me fired,* he thought. *If I follow Dr. Arthur's instructions, Ella will be angry. If I follow Ella's instructions, Dr. Arthur will be angry. Which one should I listen to? Or maybe neither one. . . .*

TRANSITIONS

Transitions was a methadone maintenance program designed to administer methadone to individuals with opiate dependence. Transitions' staff included a medical director, a registered pharmacist, nurses, and certified clinical counselors. The purpose of the program was to help patients reduce or cease the

1. Development of this decision case was supported in part by funding from the University of South Carolina College of Social Work. It was prepared solely to provide material for class discussion and not to suggest either effective or ineffective handling of the situation depicted. While based on field research regarding an actual situation, names and certain facts may have been disguised to protect confidentiality. The author and editors wish to thank the anonymous case reporter for his cooperation in making this account available for the benefit of social work students and instructors. Copyright © 2005 Thomson Learning.

abuse of other drugs related to the lifestyle of opiate dependency such as cocaine, amphetamines, methamphetamine, alcohol, and benzodiazepines. Patients were "stabilized" on methadone so that they could begin a reduction in "risky behaviors" such as IV drug use, purchasing and selling illegal or controlled substances, and general criminal activity intended to support their opiate dependency. Working with their counselors, patients were referred to local area mental health facilities or programs, inpatient treatment centers, intensive outpatient treatment centers, physicians skilled in treating the medical disorders common in opiate patients, and/or organizations related to vocational rehabilitation. Patients and counselors also constructed a treatment plan that was updated every 90 days to help the patient focus on issues that may contribute to or be the direct result of drug abuse. Patients' goals were usually related to employment, family dynamics, spirituality, and psychopathology. The staff hoped that patients would use their time on methadone to rebuild their lives and to maintain sobriety. Time in treatment was highly individual due to each patient's need. Some patients entered the program to detox from opiates while others were required to be on methadone for the rest of their lives.

To Kerry, Transitions still felt very much like the new methadone maintenance program it was—maybe newer. The program had opened only a few months before, and the staff was still regrouping from having spent the first 2 months operating under the wrong set of regulations. They still felt very cautious, checking and rechecking themselves and each other, relearning, and arguing about policies and procedures. Dr. Gwyneth Arthur, an internist and trained addictions specialist, opened Transitions in March with a silent business partner, making Transitions the second methadone maintenance program in Athens, Georgia. She was new at the administrative aspects of managing an entire program, rather than just the medical services she had been directing at the Pines Community Hospital substance abuse treatment unit. So, Dr. Arthur had been dismayed to hear from her new program director, Bill Preston, that DHEC had sent them an obsolete and more lenient set of regulations regarding policies and procedures for the administration and dispensing of methadone. The first couple of months Transitions was open, patients had been granted privileges under policies that were considerably more flexible than those put in place following Bill's discovery in May. That 2-month period was long enough for word to get out on the street that some regulations were more lenient, so some newer patients were more than a little disgruntled at some of the changed rules they had to follow.

A CAST OF "CHARACTERS"

Dr. Gwyneth Arthur wasn't all that happy about some of the rules, either—or rules in general, for that matter. She considered a good many of them just arbitrary, and took pleasure in flaunting some she considered especially silly—dress codes at the hospital, for instance. Some days she could be mistaken for one of the clients coming and going from Transitions or the hospital outpatient clinic. A tall and big-boned woman, in jeans and flannel shirts, hiking boots, heavy grey braids, and no jewelry or makeup, she could look rather rough around the edges, but clients from all walks of life—from street people to highly educated powerful people—seemed comfortable with her. Somehow, her direct, even blunt, way of speaking, laced liberally with expletives and sarcasm, seemed not to offend clients, although it could keep other people a little off balance at times. She had set a high standard at the hospital for her level of direct involvement with clients, making rounds every day, and her personal commitment to clients was just as evident at Transitions.

Bill Preston, RN, the program director, brought considerable experience and a real knack for making sense of the hundreds of regulations—federal, state, and those of various insurance companies—that governed a methadone program like Transitions. As Kerry became more familiar with the staff, he began to realize that despite Bill's distinct lack of "people skills" and the many ways he could irritate, even offend, staff and clients alike, he really was invaluable to Dr. Arthur. He had probably saved Transitions from serious problems, both financially and with regulators, by realizing so promptly that the regulations they were implementing were not the most current ones for the type of program they were operating. Kerry had decided early to stay out of the staff's breakroom complaint sessions about Bill, and concentrated on understanding Bill's perspectives on the work they were doing. Kerry found himself smiling from time to time at Bill's jeans-and-tees attire, his pride in the vintage Porsche he drove, and his absolute commitment to leave work on time to get back to Conyers for his kids' ballgames and band concerts: *not your average suit-and-tie, stick-in-the-mud administrator-type,* he'd had to acknowledge.

Ella Markham, LISW, had come from another drug treatment program in the city to be the clinical director at Transitions. Kerry had known a little about her, by reputation, even before he applied to work in the new program. Her appearance—her willowy 6-foot height, the peasant garb she wore most days, and the very long jet-black hair that she wore perfectly straight—made her quite memorable visually. The little tidbits she shared about former clients she'd served—people with extreme dissociative disorder, borderline personality disorder, paranoid schizophrenia, domestic violence, always something dramatic—made her memorable professionally, too. Kerry had been more than a little surprised the first time he entered Ella's office for supervision—pillows on the floor, incense burning, music playing softly, lamps draped with scarves to soften the lighting. "I just cannot bear the cold, clinical atmosphere of this building—at least I can make my own space a little more personal," she told him.

KERRY CARSON

Kerry's route to having earned an MSW was not exactly conventional. From a well-established career as an independent graphic artist for major national publications, through 2 years at a Trappist monastery and 10 years studying with an elderly Central American shaman, to the recent months he had spent caring for a friend as he died of cancer, Kerry had explored several possibilities for a new direction for his life. The door into social work had opened most readily, so that was the choice he'd made, but the doors out of graduate school into the professional world of work were more limited than he had imagined. His experiences in mental health and substance abuse treatment during and since school had not yet afforded him the opportunity to integrate his personal and spiritual perspectives into his professional work. There just weren't the support and openness he felt he would need in order to attempt it, and he was still coming to grips with his disappointment about that.

Kerry was a new MSW graduate at 45, but field placement supervisors had been impressed with his considerable life experience and his settled, calm demeanor. He had established a strong track record in those field placements and the jobs he'd worked at while in school—a hospital emergency room, a neuro-psychiatry unit, a psychiatric hospital, and a substance abuse outpatient treatment center. He had hoped for work more along the lines of a hospice or something of that sort but, saddled with student loans he wanted to get out from under as quickly as possible, Kerry was ready to get to work.

Kerry's job interview at Transitions had reflected the unsettled, still-evolving environment and staff relationships in the new program, and he had withdrawn his application the following day. But Ella had been persistent, saying she wanted another MSW there, someone with mental health experience. She had asked him to reconsider, pushed to get him hired, and then taken him under her wing during his first couple of months there, offering support and occasionally rides to or from work on rainy days.

But 3 months later he was still trying to figure out Ella, working to make sense of the inconsistencies he observed in her—he was a little puzzled by what seemed to him a "disconnect" between the cozy nest she had created in her office and the person he saw in all-out fights over minutia in staff meetings. He was uncomfortable with the things she told him about other staff members during their supervisory sessions and with her obvious hostility toward Bill, the program director. His discomfort had increased notably the day she asked him for a mental health referral for her boyfriend, with the condition that wherever he went she wanted him to sign a release to allow her to be involved in his treatment. "He's an alcoholic and very depressed so he's not a reliable reporter of his own condition," Ella told Kerry. That's odd, Kerry thought, uneasy about Ella's making a request like that. Her long and rambling description of her relationship, peppered with frequent hints at abuse and rape in her past, also added to his discomfort. Too much disclosure, Kerry thought, and too soon in our relationship.

He was also still unsure, 3 months into the new job, about whether it had been a good decision for him to take the position. Kerry really enjoyed his work with a few of his clients—the ones who desired some insight into their drug use, and seemed to have some internal motivation to change. But he often found himself baffled and frustrated by others who continued behaviors learned through years of addiction—manipulation, intimidation, mistrust of compassion, lying out of habit, and the desire for instant gratification. Unfortunately for him, these clients were in the majority. Staff referred to the most difficult ones as "stone cold addicts." They were the ones who were always in crisis, consistently relapsing, and pushing the limits—constantly looking for ways around the rules. Sometimes Kerry felt more like a cop than a counselor. He was uncomfortable with the level of confrontation that seemed to be expected and necessary to work with these clients—it just felt so foreign and false to him. He listened to the other counselors tell "war stories"— looking for interventions that were fair, compassionate, but firm—and said to himself, I've got to get tougher.

TWO OF KERRY'S CLIENTS

Kerry inherited some clients from another therapist—Don Ormond—who had lasted only a couple of months at Transitions, and he was still figuring out his own assessment of their issues and progress to date. Greg Ross was one of these clients, and one of the more challenging puzzles for him.

Greg had been among the first clients to come to Transitions right after it opened. Kerry had learned from Don's assessment that Greg came in because of 3 years of narcotic abuse, reportedly using more than 160 mg of OxyContin a day. He had originally started using OxyContin because of pain from a back injury at work, but he had developed a massive tolerance for the drug, and the amount he had claimed to need to control his pain had escalated sharply. He had presented a prescription when he first came to Transitions to prove he was using OxyContin legally, so that his positive screens wouldn't set off alarms with the staff, but he was evasive about signing a release for Dr. Arthur to contact his orthopedist. Around the time Don left, he had just begun to realize, and had documented it as a question, that Greg was not telling his orthopedic doctor about the methadone, but rather just adding it to the still-significant level of OxyContin the doctor would continue to prescribe for him. Some staff even suspected him of selling some of his OxyContin on the street to fund his habit. Four 40 mg tablets of OxyContin—a day's supply—could bring up to $320 on the street. For someone living on disability payments, Greg always seemed to have money. He often talked about the expansion of his land in the country, and he drove an expensive SUV.

Kerry had been amazed the first time he met Greg to see no obvious signs of the huge dose of narcotic he was taking. His eyes, gait, and speech—everything seemed normal. And that first time was not a fluke—Greg just never seemed "snowed." During the first month or two that Kerry worked with him, Greg seemed to be doing fairly well—very cooperative, punctual for appointments, no other drugs present in his tests other than the ones prescribed for him—although his flat affect was disconcerting. He just never smiled. But then he began to seem shaky, evasive, labile, and would address Kerry with an eerie sense of entitlement. He had contracted with Dr. Arthur to begin titrating (reducing gradually) his OxyContin, but Greg's drug levels—that were supposed to be gradually tapering down—had been at a plateau for the last 3 weeks. Greg's adherence to OxyContin was puzzling. Methadone blocks the euphoria of other opiates, a side effect that made it valuable in long-term behavior modification. Methadone patients cannot tell the difference between IV morphine and IV saline once they have reached a therapeutic dose. Kerry wondered, "Why is he still taking OxyContin. He never seems to be in pain."

Unlike Greg, Julia Ruiz entered treatment shortly after Kerry was employed. She was the fifth patient to be added to his caseload. Kerry completed Julia's chemical dependency assessment with her and oriented her to the clinic policies and procedures. She had never been in methadone treatment before and she came voluntarily to Transitions on a Friday late in August. Born in Guatemala, but adopted when she was 5 years old by a single professional woman in Georgia, Julia had lived most of her 20 years in the United States, and had almost no Spanish accent. At Kerry's first session with her, it was plain that she had been in trouble with drugs for quite some time—she was painfully thin, her nose was running and her eyes were teary, she had visible sores on her wrists and ankles, and she couldn't hide the restlessness that was so characteristic of withdrawal. As he began to ask about her history, he learned that she had been treated in more than one residential facility for substance abuse and mental health problems, in other states as well as Georgia. He learned that she had a preference for heroin and cocaine, and that she always took her drugs intravenously.

The longer they talked, the more concerned Kerry became. Julia's adoptive mother had died suddenly only 6 weeks before Julia's intake visit, and she was overwhelmed with the loss and with the tasks involved in sorting out her mother's estate. Gradually Kerry pieced together her cautious responses to questions, learning that she had a job in a restaurant and a Mexican boyfriend. The boyfriend, Jose, was an immigrant with no documentation and was dependent on her for housing, food, and translation. He had been arrested several times for domestic violence, but Julia always dropped the charges when he called begging for another chance. And Kerry learned that prior to Julia's adoption she had been "in the system" of child welfare, living with foster families. In response to his questions about whether she had experienced any physical, emotional, or sexual abuse in foster care, she said flatly, "all of that."

Pausing for a moment to collect his thoughts, Kerry asked, "Julia, would you be more comfortable with a female counselor? I would be glad to arrange that for you if it would make things any easier."

"No, I prefer a male counselor," she said firmly. Julia was experiencing withdrawal from opiates and was clearly uncomfortable, and Kerry was reluctant to probe too deeply into her reasons at this early tentative stage of treatment. Not sure what her preference would mean in their work together, Kerry asked if it would be okay if he left the door to his office open, and Julia nodded her assent.

As he watched Julia walk down the hall after their first session, Kerry had to attend to the anxiety he was feeling. *She's not well at all. I don't see a reason to forcibly hospitalize her and she doesn't want to go, but I don't feel good about her leaving. But, she did come in on her own, and that's positive. I just hope she comes back.*

But when the results of her drug screening urine and blood work came in later that afternoon, worry got the upper hand again—not only was Julia positive for heroin and cocaine, she was also positive for hepatitis C—the result of years of IV drug use. And she was pregnant. *I wonder if she knows?* Kerry thought. *Of all the things I thought about when I took this job, having to tell a woman I just met that she is pregnant was not one of them!*

MONDAY

The following Monday, Julia came for her appointment as scheduled, but she appeared to be in intense physical pain; she could barely walk and sitting wasn't much better. Her arms were covered in bruises and one side of her face was swollen. Once again, Kerry was careful as he questioned her, not wanting to push her too hard yet. *We need to talk about the pregnancy and the hepatitis,* he thought, *but she's in bad shape.* Eventually, he learned that Jose had thrown Julia through the front door of their apartment over the weekend. He was in jail. Kerry challenged her not to drop the charges this time, pushing her to confront the facts of the increasing severity of her injuries. At first Julia was hesitant, saying that things between them had been getting better, but finally she agreed to go through with the process this time. He offered her some community resources, to provide support while she was dealing with so many changes, and to help her develop a plan for when Jose got out of jail.

"I'll think about it," was all Julia would agree to.

That may be a pretty significant step for her, just to think about it, Kerry thought. *But at least she's real, not playing games, and she's willing to consider making some changes. That makes all the difference in how I feel about working with her.*

In the first of his afternoon appointments, Kerry was sharply reminded of the contrast between Julia and some of his other clients. Greg's screen came back positive for cocaine and benzodiazepines. He reluctantly admitted to Kerry that his wife had demanded he move out of the house and she intended to file for divorce, because she had learned that he was riding to the clinic with one of the other clients and having an affair with her. But Greg insisted to Kerry—quite firmly—that he was taking only the drugs that were ordered for him.

"Greg, your 'legal' drug levels have not shown any improvement for weeks, and now there's cocaine and benzo in your urine. You've obviously been using, and we need to talk about it." Kerry tried to reason with Greg, just wanting him to be straight about what he was doing.

"Your lab is wrong, and I can prove it. Because that's not been my urine for the last 3 weeks. I got my 4-year-old nephew to pee in a cup for me, and you've been testing his urine and not even knowing it. I know my nephew's not using cocaine and benzos, so your lab is incompetent," Greg said with a satisfied smile.

Kerry was dumbfounded. Greg had just confessed to an act that could get him administratively discharged from the clinic—diversion of urine. As the doctor always said, "Flunking a urine test is sick behavior, but cheating on a urine test is just bad behavior." Kerry couldn't decide whether to laugh or yell or argue or have Greg thrown out of the center. *Is he insane? Does he really expect people to believe that? Why would he think that's better than just admitting he's been using?* Kerry needed time to regroup and to consult with someone. "Greg, I'm going to have to get back to you about that. This is obviously a very important matter, and I'm going to make an appointment for you to see the doctor so you can discuss our testing with her. She is certified in drug testing. Go on and get your dose at the pharmacy, and I'll see you when you come on Wednesday."

TUESDAY

On Tuesday morning, Kerry and Ella met to go over his cases. He told her about what had happened to Julia. He had hardly gotten the facts out, let alone any of his thinking about how to proceed with her, when Ella jumped in: "You need to notify the authorities—this is child abuse."

Kerry wasn't sure where she was headed with this. "There's no child—she's 20."

"She's pregnant, and she's using drugs. You have to report it," Ella insisted.

"Ella, I don't think drug use during pregnancy has to be reported, not yet anyway," Kerry responded, feeling very uneasy about Ella's directive. "And she seems really skittish about being here, even though it's by her own choice. I'm afraid if I violate her confidentiality now, she won't come back."

"Kerry, I'm telling you, report it *now*." Her tone was emphatic, and her voice was getting louder. "You could lose your license if you don't."

"I'll consider it," Kerry said and opened another folder. He began to tell her about Greg and his claim that he had used his nephew's urine in his last three urine screens. Ella hardly let him finish the sentence before she jumped in again:

"You need to report him," she said, "for child abuse." This time, he decided not to even try to discuss it with her, and simply nodded and closed the chart, thankful when Ella started right in on another matter.

After their meeting, when Ella had headed back to her office, Kerry checked, and Dr. Arthur's door was open, so he knocked lightly on the door-jamb. "Do you have a minute?"

"Sure, Kerry, what's up?" Dr. Arthur turned around from her desk to face him. "Well, I just had a supervision session with Ella, and she said I need to report *two* of my clients for child abuse, but I'm not so sure." Kerry went on to describe what was happening with Julia, concluding with "she says she's not going to back off the charges against Jose this time, so I think she's safe from him for right now. And I thought we didn't have to report drug use by a pregnant woman until late in the pregnancy. Julia is only about 3 months pregnant—she just found out. I really hate to report it right now—she came here on her own and wants to get straightened out, and she just seems so fragile—I'd rather wait and see how she does for a little while. I don't think there's any threat of immediate harm that's going to be different if we wait a few days to staff it with the treatment team."

"Don't do anything yet, Kerry—I think you're right, give it a little time and see what develops. No point getting the legal system involved if we don't have to, and if it won't do her any good."

"And then there's Greg. I was trying to get him to acknowledge he was using, because his screen came back positive for coke and benzo, and he was denying it, said the lab must have made a mistake. Maybe I pushed too hard, because all of a sudden he got all red in the face and said he could prove he wasn't using, because he'd been substituting his 4-year-old nephew's urine the last three times. I have to admit, I was so stunned by that I didn't know *what* to say! But Ella says that's abusing the nephew, and I have to report it."

Shaking her head and laughing quietly, Dr. Arthur replied, "I don't think so, because it's so damned preposterous. All we need is to have the clinic sued by this guy. When he comes in tomorrow, you can just do an observed collection of his urine specimen, and have *him* do the test strip in front of you—and better have a witness, just in case. That will put an end to the nephew story."

"Okay, thanks. I'll let you know if things change, and we can talk about it in staffing."

Kerry was relieved—until mid-afternoon when he saw Ella in the hall. "Did you make those reports yet?" she demanded.

"Dr. Arthur said to hold off a bit—we don't have to report yet," he responded, dreading what Ella would say to that.

"I gave you a direct order to report it, Kerry. Why did you go to Dr. Arthur?"

"I just think we need to talk about it some more, not rush into it, and Dr. Arthur agreed."

"Fine—I will take this up with her, and I'll talk to you later," she snapped, and turned away.

THE WEDNESDAY FROM . . .

To his relief, he didn't hear anything more—until mid-afternoon the next day, when he found an e-mail from Ella, directing him to transfer Julia to her case-load, moments before Julia was scheduled for a session. Shocked, he sat staring at the message—and then Julia knocked at his office door. She looked even worse, if possible—the bruises on her face had begun to show, and she was clearly guarding her ribs, breathing cautiously—in fact, everything about her seemed cautious. But she said she was ready to get some other help, and she signed a release for Kerry to refer her to Safe Homes.

"You can go on over to the pharmacy and get your dose," he suggested, "and then come back here and I should have some information for you." Kerry moved to the door with Julia, and watched her start down the hall.

Just then Ella came out of her office, hesitated just for a moment, then walked up to Julia and took her by the arm.

"You need to come with me," she said, and started back toward her office. Julia shot Kerry a look of confusion and pleading. Horrified, Kerry hurried toward them.

"Julia was just going over to get her dose, and then I need for her to come back and finish with me."

Ella took Julia by the arm and pulled her into her office, then turned to Kerry and said, "you can come in or stay out, I don't care which," and started to shut the door.

Feeling really lame but worried about Julia, Kerry put his hand out to keep her from completely closing the door, pushed it back open, and went in.

"Ella is my supervisor, Julia," he said, responding to the alarm and questions in Julia's eyes, just as Ella began bombarding Julia with a series of questions.

"Tell me about this abuse you said you have experienced—how old were you? You were adopted when you were 5 years old—how sure are you, really, about these very serious allegations you've made? Why are you risking your baby's health with all these drugs you're doing? Don't you know we will have to report you to DSS?" Tears began to spill from Julia's eyes.

Kerry knew he was about to lose his temper with Ella and say something inappropriate, so he stood up, said "I really need to finish my session with Julia right now, Ella," and he opened the door and stood between it and Ella so that Julia could exit in front of him.

Once they were back in his office, he closed the door and turned to Julia. "What just happened in there, Julia, will not ever happen in this office. I'm so sorry. I hope you will come back," he said, but thought, *though I wouldn't blame you for a second if you don't, not after that.* She said she would, but Kerry wasn't sure he believed her, and wondered as she left if he would ever see her again.

Tense and utterly frustrated, Kerry Carson put on his reflector vest and helmet, unlocked his bike, and headed for home, feeling he couldn't get away from Transitions fast enough. Weaving his way through traffic faster than usual, he had to remind himself to pay attention to what he was doing and not to get lost in sorting out this bewildering day. Once at home, he sank onto the floor and leaned back against the sofa, and let the thoughts flow through him. *What in the world is going on? And what am I doing caught in the middle of it? Maybe I was right, that it's not a good fit for me there—but getting stuck between Dr. Arthur and Ella and possibly getting myself fired sure wasn't what I had in mind. And which one of them should I listen to about reporting Julia? What am I supposed to do about alleged abuse, if you can call it that, if I am fired? I've got to find a way to make some sense out of all this, figure out what it means for me—I don't want to come home every afternoon feeling like I may explode.*

Case 9

I Don't Know How
It Happened[1]

JULIE E. SPRINKLE

It was a typical Thursday afternoon in April 2002 at Greater Cincinnati Home Health Care.

Janet Reid, director of social work, had just returned from a late lunch and was sorting through a stack of paperwork. Sighing to herself, she bemoaned the seemingly endless barrage of administrative tasks and responsibilities.

Around 2:30 P.M., Marcy Bishop stopped by Janet's office and asked, "Can I talk to you?"

Because it was common practice for staff members to stop by for a quick consultation, Janet assumed that Marcy had something routine to discuss. When Marcy closed the door, however, Janet knew that this would not be an ordinary conversation; this was serious.

After some hesitation and wringing of hands, Marcy finally spoke. "I need to tell you something that I think you may have to fire me over."

1. Development of this decision case was supported in part by funding from the University of South Carolina College of Social Work. It was prepared solely to provide material for class discussion and not to suggest either effective or ineffective handling of the situation depicted. While based on field research regarding an actual situation, names and certain facts may have been disguised to protect confidentiality. The author and editors wish to thank the anonymous case reporter for her cooperation in making this account available for the benefit of social work students and instructors. Copyright © 2005 Thomson Learning.

GREATER CINCINNATI HOME
HEALTH CARE

Greater Cincinnati Home Health Care (GCHHC) began serving clients in the late 1970s. The nonprofit agency provided comprehensive home nursing and rehabilitation services to residents in three counties in southern Ohio and two adjacent counties in Kentucky—a large service area that included small communities and rural farming areas in addition to Cincinnati itself. Although it had become quite large, employing more than 200 health care professionals, it had maintained a reputation for personalized, compassionate, expert care that it had built in its early days.

Janet Reid had come to GCHHC approximately 7 years earlier. At that time, she was in her mid-30s and had just completed an MSW degree. She also held a master's degree in religious education from a Presbyterian seminary. Since becoming director of the social work department 2 years earlier, Janet supervised 20 social workers. Her assistant, Sylvia Albanese, usually did more of the clinical supervision, while Janet handled more of the administrative aspects, although each of them readily covered for the other. Janet truly loved her work and appreciated her staff—a cohesive group, despite some of the growing pains of recent years.

Marcy Bishop, a social worker in her late 50s, began working at GCHHC soon after Janet did. She and Janet were social workers on the same home health teams, first pediatrics and then adults, for several years, and they always had a good relationship. Janet's promotion to a supervisory role was not an issue between the two women; in fact, Marcy had urged her to pursue it. Marcy was raised Catholic, but was not currently practicing. She had four grown children and couldn't wait to be a grandmother. Her second divorce had become final 2 years before.

Janet thought of Marcy as a "wonderful, wonderful social worker." She had a genuine ability to focus on what her patients needed and to see beyond the surface. Patients were often hostile or angry, yet Marcy took it all in stride. Friends and coworkers viewed her as articulate, conceptually sophisticated, and very creative. According to Janet, "She's the kind of person you could say anything to, and she would see it in the most positive light."

Ed Baxter had been the executive director of GCHHC for 3 years, and the agency had grown tremendously under his leadership, more than tripling its average daily census. He had insisted on reorganization so that new patients could be admitted and seen by their team members within 24 hours of referral, rather than the 48 hours that had been their previous goal. He had demanded far greater cost-consciousness of all staff members than was customary—a painful culture change for some staff, but eased because he allocated the savings to increased services for patients and their families.

Janet had had several arguments with her new boss over how staff matters should be handled. Ed tended to focus on measurable, specific behaviors, and to be rather punitive, while Janet placed more emphasis on the qualitative, subjective aspects of an employee's performance, and worked to help her staff continue their professional and personal development. Ed had precipitously fired a chaplain on the pediatrics team the year before on hearing of an ongoing relationship between the chaplain and the mother of a child on his caseload.

THE INCIDENT

Because she believed Marcy was an excellent social worker, only something really terrible could make Janet consider firing Marcy. From the look on Marcy's face, Janet had a sinking feeling she was about to hear something really terrible.

With only a nod from Janet, Marcy blurted, "I spent the weekend with a patient's daughter and I think there's a chance I've been exposed to HIV."

Struggling to comprehend what Marcy had just disclosed, Janet encouraged Marcy to tell her story, starting from the beginning. Marcy spoke almost nonstop. Janet just listened.

Marcy told Janet things began about 6 weeks before, when Marcy was assigned a new client, Ted Schwartz. Ted and his wife, Jean, were a pleasant couple in their mid-60s. Their only daughter, Lisa, arrived from California shortly after Ted became a client at GCHHC. Lisa had made plans to stay in the area in order to be near her dad, even going so far as to rent an apartment for herself. Marcy said she thought Lisa was an interesting, seemingly free-spirited person and that both the interaction between Lisa and her father and the way Lisa was handling her father's serious illness impressed her. Marcy had several routine conversations with Lisa while at the Schwartz's home.

Then, Marcy continued, "Lisa called me, in tears, at 5 o'clock the Friday afternoon before last. I assumed she was confronting grief issues and wanted to talk about her father's illness." Lisa asked Marcy if they could meet. Marcy readily agreed and headed over to Lisa's apartment.

"When I arrived at Lisa's apartment, Lisa was no longer crying." Wondering why she had been asked to come over, Marcy began asking questions to learn what had prompted Lisa's tearful phone call. At first, Lisa kept the conversation light and casual. To better understand Lisa, Marcy started probing Lisa about her family. Marcy said, "As Lisa talked, she got this trance-like look in her eyes. She spoke slowly and softly—her voice changed, and she sounded . . . well, she sounded younger. She eventually described what I would call ritual sexual abuse that happened when she was a child. She didn't say who did it."

Janet noticed that Marcy started to speak methodically, as if in a slight trance herself. Janet then remembered that Marcy had recently begun attending a support group for individuals who experienced "quasi" sexual abuse as children, such as ritual enemas or invasive touching. But Janet said nothing, and Marcy continued.

"After recounting the abuse, Lisa stopped talking, 'zoned out,' and then," Marcy hesitated before continuing, "she appeared to have a flashback. She didn't seem to know that I was in the room. She began to cry and tremble, and turned her head to one side. She also threw up her hands, as if defending herself from someone. It seemed very real to me."

Marcy admitted that she was simultaneously horrified by Lisa's admission and distressed by her behavior. In an effort to soothe the emotionally distraught woman, Marcy said she spoke softly to Lisa and patiently waited for her to "come back." After what seemed like an eternity, Lisa appeared to reorient to time and place.

"Lisa physically turned to me for comfort. I placed my arms around her and held her silently." Marcy swallowed hard, looked down at her hands, and then back at Janet. "Then she started kissing me. And then we had sex. I don't know how this happened. I can't believe it happened. I can't believe I did this." Looking completely miserable, Marcy went on to explain that she spent the weekend at Lisa's apartment. After a very intense weekend punctuated by cycles of conversation and intimacy, Marcy left Lisa's apartment Monday morning to go home and get ready for work. As she spoke, Marcy's voice was shaking and her face was pale.

"While I was getting ready for work, the whole thing hit me. I immediately called Lisa and told her I was sorry but that I couldn't do this. I wanted to be upfront and not drag it out. Lisa was furious! She screamed at me, blasting me with a whole string of scathing accusations—that I had used her, that I was cruel, things like that. She kind of scared me, but I didn't know anything else to do, and didn't think I could talk to anyone about it."

Taking a breath, Marcy continued. "Later that same week, I went on a routine visit to Ted's house. Ted and Jean informed me that Lisa had left town in a whirlwind, with absolutely no explanation. Much to my relief, they did not know why she had gone, or appear to have any idea about what had happened between Lisa and me. Ted told me that this type of behavior was 'typical Lisa' and that he and Jean had long since come to terms with her instability and the fact that they were powerless to control her flighty behavior. Ted spontaneously added that Lisa had a history of telling people that she had been sexually abused as a child in order to gain their sympathy, but that he did not believe there was any truth to her allegations. I didn't disclose that Lisa had already relayed these accounts of ritual abuse." Marcy paused. "Janet, he seems like a nice man, but I couldn't help wondering if he had been the one who abused her, and was doing the usual denial and blame-the-victim thing."

"Anyway, Ted continued to talk about Lisa's history, and he said that Lisa was 'pretty promiscuous.' I tried to remain focused on what Ted was saying, but my mind started racing. I was horrified! If she's from California and promiscuous, there's a pretty good chance she's been exposed to HIV. So that means I might have been exposed to HIV!"

Marcy told Janet that she had struggled with her conscience for almost 2 weeks. She said she knew that her behavior was out of line and that the chaplain had been fired for a similar infraction. "I can't stop thinking about the possibility of HIV. If I'm HIV positive, it will be apparent to everyone that I engaged in a relationship with Lisa."

Janet sat silently, floored by Marcy's admission of sexual involvement with a patient's daughter and the possibility that she might have been exposed to HIV in the process. Marcy pulled her back into the moment by asking, "What should I do? Should I change cases and no longer be Ted's social worker? What can I do to make this situation better?" As Janet carefully weighed her response, Marcy prodded, "You'll have to tell Ed, won't you?"

Case 10

How Can Everyone Get
a Just Share?[1]

KAREN A. GRAY
TERRY A. WOLFER

n late January 2002, Malcolm Little, executive director of Just Share, left the House Ways and Means Health and Human Services subcommittee meeting feeling heavyhearted. With South Carolina's $320 million revenue shortfall, agencies were being forced to cut their budgets once again. For Health and Human Services, this meant deciding whether to cut Medicaid services for children or for the elderly. Frustration and anger welled up, as Malcolm reflected, "This is the second year of budget cuts, and most agencies have cut what little fat they had from their budgets. More cuts will mean cutting muscle. That 'muscle' is vital services to citizens of our state. We need to decide how Just Share can weigh in on the issues, and quick, while there's still time to

1. Development of this decision case was supported in part by funding from the University of South Carolina College of Social Work. It was prepared solely to provide material for class discussion and not to suggest either effective or ineffective handling of the situation depicted. While based on field research regarding an actual situation, names and certain facts may have been disguised to protect confidentiality. The authors and editors wish to thank the anonymous case reporter for his cooperation in making this account available for the benefit of social work students and instructors. Revised from an appendix in Wolfer, T. A., & Gray, K. A. (forthcoming). Using the decision case method to teach legislative policy advocacy. *Journal of Teaching in Social Work*. Article copies available from the Haworth Document Delivery Service: 1-800-HAWORTH. E-mail address: docdelivery@haworthpress.com. Copyright © 2005 Haworth Press.

exert some influence. Children and elderly folks' lives might be literally on the line."

JUST SHARE

Just Share, a statewide consumer advocacy organization, was founded 15 years before to protect the everyday citizen/consumer in South Carolina. A "consumer" was defined as anyone who consumed governmental services, pharmaceuticals, utilities, public transportation, or financial services. However, Just Share focused on low and moderate-income families because they spend such a large portion of their income on essential goods and services (i.e., food and utilities). As Malcolm described it, "Our mission is to enhance the health, safety, and well-being of everyday people in the Palmetto state; which is a very bland way to say that we're about building the infrastructure for a social change movement in South Carolina."

In order of organizational priority, Just Share's activities included community organizing, policy advocacy that included lobbying on behalf of low-income consumers, and training for grassroots community organizations. Although Just Share did not do casework, they routinely received phone calls from individual consumers. In such cases, they typically referred people to appropriate agencies or to an attorney. As Malcolm explained, the organization's activities and issues "are more staff directed than board directed."

According to Malcolm, "Our bylaws state that it is imperative that the majority of our board should be people of color and women. Currently we only have one white male, a local trial lawyer." There were 11 board members; they included the executive director of the state labor board, the director of Multifaith Community Services, two professors from the University of South Carolina, and four consumers, such as an uninsured undergraduate student at Columbia College.

Although Just Share had developed an effective presence with state government, the state legislature, and local communities, it was a small organization. The three other staff members included Tim Flannery, PhD, Research Director (part-time), who had been with the organization from the beginning; Dana Glover, MSW, Program Associate who had been on staff for nearly 2 years; and Christy Tucker, Development Director, a fund-raiser who was also a recent addition. According to Malcolm, raising money was sometimes difficult because, "We piss people off. We usually take the position that others are afraid to take, such as advocating for same sex marriages and outlawing marital rape." Most funding (80 percent) came from national foundations (outside of South Carolina). The remaining funds came from a local foundation and individual contributions by 350 in-state members of Just Share. The annual budget was approximately $200,000.

MALCOLM LITTLE, MSW

Not quite 30 years old, Malcolm had several years experience in community organizing and advocacy in South Carolina and other states. An ex-football player for the University of South Carolina, he had an imposing physical presence. This, coupled with his charisma, intelligence, and warmth, made him someone that people remembered long after meeting him. As an African American man from a working-class background, several experiences had contributed to his passion for social justice. While Malcolm was growing up, his father was in the military and his mother was a teacher. Nevertheless, his family still qualified for food stamps. It angered Malcolm that his parents worked so hard and were so woefully underpaid. Malcolm recounted how his undergraduate years helped form his feelings about justice: "I was oppressed and exploited as a Division I college football player. I participated in a sport that generated several million dollars a week for a university, but I personally didn't have money to buy toothpaste, deodorant, clothes, or shoes for myself. Other black men and I were physically, emotionally, and financially exploited by big-money college athletics and given little to nothing in return. We were left with a degree, if we got one at all, that wasn't even worth the paper it was printed on. After I graduated from college, I worked for minimum wage for 18 months."

Although very good at building relationships, Malcolm wasn't afraid of confrontation. His curiosity, imagination, and passion—other qualities important for a community organizer and policy advocate—sometimes led him to take on too much. Malcolm knew this limited his effectiveness because he didn't always have enough time to devote to all of Just Share's projects.

THE STATE OF THE STATE

In the 1990s, during an extended period of relative prosperity and budget surpluses, South Carolina legislators had passed, and a Democratic governor had signed, several major tax cuts. But in late 2001, for the second year in a row, South Carolina experienced a budget crisis when shrinking tax revenues from a slumping economy could not keep pace with state budget needs.

Therefore, this year coming up with a budget was going to be a painful, arduous, and dividing process. All budget bills originated in the solidly Republican House; if passed, the bills move onto the Senate. In November 2001, all state agency directors were given specific directives before presenting their budgets to the House Ways and Means subcommittees: "Don't show up with a big budget. Trim as much as possible, and then more will be trimmed."

Rick Quinn, a Republican, the House Majority leader, and chairman of the Ways and Means subcommittee on health care said that $100 million of the cuts had to come from health care, specifically the Department of Health and Human Services that administered Medicaid. This $100 million cut would cost South Carolina approximately $400 million in reduced expenditures, because the state would lose matching federal dollars.

The total Medicaid budget for the state of South Carolina was $2.9 billion. Most of it was spent on two populations: children and elderly or disabled adults. In South Carolina, less than 6 percent of the current Medicaid population received TANF. Forty-four percent of all children (>370,000) in South Carolina received Medicaid. Medicaid paid for two-thirds of all nursing home beds and half of the births in South Carolina. If the proposed budget cuts targeted both children and the elderly or disabled adults, it could result in up to 42,000 children losing Medicaid and up to 46,000 elderly or disabled adults losing coverage for prescription drugs.

The director of the Department of Health and Human Services was John Kramer. In light of the budget crisis, he offered several proposals for the General Assembly to consider. First, he suggested South Carolina could reduce optional Medicaid services. One conservative legislator liked to call South Carolina's Medicaid program "the Cadillac version of health care" because it provided several optional services. South Carolina Medicaid covered some services because federal regulations required it to do so, and some because it chose to do so. John Kramer suggested that the state could save money by going to a bare bones Medicaid program, which meant eliminating optional services such as prescription drugs, adult day care, and Meals on Wheels. It could continue to cover hospitalization, emergency room care, and other core services as required by federal policy. Alternately, he proposed the state could reduce the number of people eligible for Medicaid, by reducing eligibility levels from 150 percent of the federal poverty level to 100 percent or by reducing nursing home coverage. But John Kramer *did not* want to reduce the amount that providers (i.e., physicians) were reimbursed for treating Medicaid patients. Because there were already too few providers, he feared a cut in reimbursement rates would prompt some providers to leave the system, thus reducing recipients' access to services.

As reported in *The State* newspaper (2002, p. A1), "Some say the cuts are politically motivated." In television ads, Democratic governor Hodges touted the Silver Card program, a prescription drug program for seniors he created the previous year. Although the program required seniors to pay a $500 deductible before they could get these prescription drug benefits, it relied on substantial funding by the state. This program was funded by part of the tobacco settlement a few years before. The $20 million from the tobacco settlement used to start the program was a "one-time shot" of funding. Thereafter, the state needed to find money to fund the program. Rick Quinn suggested scrapping the Silver Card program and funneling that $20 million into Medicaid. Under a new federal Health Insurance Portability and Accountability Act (HIPAA) proposal, it was possible to receive matching federal dollars (at a rate of 3:1) if a state extended Medicaid coverage to more seniors. This included prescription drugs and potentially recaptured 40–50 percent of the seniors cut from the Silver Card program.

JUST SHARE'S ALLIANCES
AND RELATIONSHIPS

Just Share was in coalition with several nonprofit organizations that have an interest in health care for poor children and elders. However, almost none of these organizations were positioned to act on the current crisis. For instance, NASW-SC was heavily involved in promoting a Scope of Practice bill, an effort to protect and promote the social work profession, and had little energy or resources for other issues. Statewide advocacy groups for children don't advocate for the elderly, and statewide advocacy groups for the elderly don't advocate for children. The one organization that might be in a position to advocate was a statewide legal services organization.

Both Just Share and Malcolm had a working relationship with John Kramer. He had been open to meeting with Medicaid and health care advocacy organizations on this and other issues. Malcolm knew John Kramer was in a tough position now; he didn't want to make any more cuts.

Although Just Share had productive relationships with many legislators, Rick Quinn was not one of them. As Malcolm put it, "We have influence and impact with many different legislators who are in key positions on key committees. However, we have a stumbling block with the chair of this subcommittee, Rick Quinn. Most of the organizing work Just Share does is with low and moderate-income African Americans. Quinn's constituency is moderate and high-income whites, most of whom don't see themselves in the same class as poor and middle-class black people, even though their need for quality health care is exactly the same."

FUNDING FOR HEALTH CARE

Malcolm explained Just Share's position on health care: "Health care is very important to our work at Just Share. We hung our hat on that issue in 1993 when Bill Clinton was talking about universal coverage and reforming health-care. Our recent work has mainly been to cover low-income people under Medicaid. Our primary concern is covering low-income children and their working-poor parents. We have raised money for that advocacy work. A lot of our grant proposals are tied into us having some success in organizing and affecting public policy on health care issues, which means improving public policy or changing public policy around health care. Therefore if we don't make any positive changes in health care policy this year, if seniors' and children's Medicaid services get cut then we basically have not accomplished what we were trying to do in those proposals. People understand that it is difficult to make change in that regard and that sometimes that there are 4- or 5-year fights, but funders don't fund in 4- or 5-year cycles. They fund in 1-, 2-, or possibly 3-year cycles. After the first or second year if you haven't made significant progress towards your goal then they will give the money to somebody else. Once you lose the money, you lose the momentum that you gained because you don't have money to have meetings and pay for food and child-care for these low-income people who come out in the evening and miss time off of work to come to actions or other things that we ask them to do. It puts us in a more difficult situation in order to be able to achieve anything because this is movement-building. We start with our base and build; but it takes resources to do that. It takes time to make those changes and so without the resources and without having the time to make the changes, you lose. We get a lot of our money for health care, close to $75,000. So this budget crisis is a very important issue for us, both for our constituency and for our organization."

"Do we have to decide who is more valuable—children or the elderly? Can we think outside the box? Do we have enough time and resources to think outside the box?" Malcolm mulled over his choices of actions. To him, "The choice between children and elders is a choice between primary and tertiary care, both of which are necessary for the health of South Carolina. This is the choice the subcommittee wants to make. Just Share sees other options, but these options are not palatable to many South Carolina legislators. So do we play by their rules or do we make up new rules?" The subcommittees would soon be presenting to the full committee.

Just Share thought an increase in the tobacco tax would be a good source for new revenue. A tobacco-producing state, South Carolina charged the fourth lowest amount of taxes per pack of cigarettes, only 7 cents per pack. Other states charged from 5 cents to $1.11. If South Carolina raised its tobacco tax from 7 cents per pack to 17 cents per pack, it would create $40 million in new state revenue. If South Carolina used that $40 million for a Medicaid match, it could draw down $92 million in federal dollars for a total of $130 million for Medicaid. The added benefit of increasing tobacco taxes is the inverse correlation between increased prices and decreased smoking by children. But Malcolm knew that tobacco farmers had successfully defeated such tax increases before. In addition, legislators opposed to any kind of tax increase would attempt to shoot this one down, too.

Malcolm needed to decide quickly how Just Share should weigh in.

REFERENCE

Crumbo, C. (2002, March 12). First step
    advocates plan fight. *The State,* pp. A1, A7.

Case 11

A Little Earring?![1]

HEATHER BENNETT
BRENT E. CAGLE

Elisa Price sat there staring at Charles Mitchell in disbelief. In all Elisa's years working at Greater Columbus Mental Health, she had never seen any colleague so angry, and certainly not the executive director. As Charles got up to leave and reached for the door handle, he turned to Elisa, and shouted, "If you don't find someone else, then I will!" Charles then stormed out of her office, leaving Elisa in stunned silence.

GREATER COLUMBUS MENTAL HEALTH

Greater Columbus Mental Health (GCMH) had served Columbus and the surrounding communities for more than 40 years. The agency served people with mental illness of all ages. Employing an interdisciplinary staff of psychiatrists, psychologists, and social workers, the agency provided more comprehensive care to its patients than any other mental health provider in the state.

1. Development of this decision case was supported in part by funding from the University of South Carolina College of Social Work. It was prepared solely to provide material for class discussion and not to suggest either effective or ineffective handling of the situation depicted. While based on field research regarding an actual situation, names and certain facts may have been disguised to protect confidentiality. The authors and editors wish to thank the anonymous case reporter for her cooperation in making this account available for the benefit of social work students and instructors. Copyright © 2005 Thomson Learning.

As a major part of GCMH, the Child and Family Services Department worked with children diagnosed with mental illness and their parents and siblings, as well as the children of some adult patients. The social workers within the department offered counseling services to the children and parents, in-home training with parents, education on mental illness, and case management. They also acted as advocates for children and their families in the schools and elsewhere in the community.

CHARLES MITCHELL

Charles had been executive director of GCMH for 2 years, since 1989. A former Army officer, he was white, in his mid-30s, with a receding hairline, cool blue eyes, and trim build. Charles tried hard to have a sense of humor, but he was awkward sometimes—he would laugh too loudly or just a bit too late. Very soon after coming to the agency, he tried unsuccessfully to implement a fairly strict dress code: men in jackets and ties, women in dresses or skirts with stockings and no sandals, and only occasionally dress slacks. This caused a furor among the staff. Like many directors, he had often been accused of being too focused on the "bottom line," and the staff questioned and complained about many of his budget cuts. At first, Elisa, too, was skeptical of his decisions, but she soon realized that there was a "method to his madness." It was easy to view Charles as a menace during budget meetings as he cut overhead costs down to the bone, but Elisa saw the justification for those cuts as he put those savings back into the budget for badly needed staff positions.

ELISA PRICE

Elisa, too, was white and in her mid-30s. In contrast to Charles, Elisa was easygoing and had many friends in the agency. Prior to becoming the director of Child and Family Services, Elisa was a staff social worker in the department for 5 years, and a volunteer before that. When the director's position became open, many of Elisa's fellow social workers encouraged her to apply. Although she was happy doing casework, Elisa applied and Charles gave her the job. Elisa began working as the director of Child and Family Services in October 1990.

One of Elisa's primary duties as director was to maintain an adequate staff to provide a stable level of services for the community's children and families. There was not a great deal of staff turnover at the agency, but when someone left, or when the census grew significantly, Elisa conducted initial interviews with potential hires, and then made a recommendation to her supervisor, Charles, about who should be hired. He wanted to interview the final candidate before an offer was made, but normally the hiring process went quite smoothly, and Elisa's recommendations had not been questioned thus far. In her brief time as supervisor, they had hired three other social workers before a play therapist position opened.

INTERVIEWING TO HIRE

One special service offered by the Child and Family Services Department was play therapy. In play therapy, therapists helped children problem solve and work through their emotions using artistic means (e.g., puppets, toys, artwork). One of the two play therapists had left her position to move to Chicago, leaving Elisa with the duty of hiring a new therapist.

Keenly aware of the contributions made by the play therapists, Elisa was anxious to find a replacement. She began interviewing potential candidates on Monday, but by the end of the week Elisa felt more than a little discouraged about the prospects. She had one last interview scheduled for Friday afternoon, and by this point Elisa was praying for a miracle.

Jeff Gergen arrived for his interview on time, and he and Elisa quickly established a rapport with one another. Jeff was neatly but informally dressed, which Elisa felt was appropriate if he were working with children. He had a bright smile that made him seem younger than 27 years old or so, a guess Elisa based on his various graduation dates. Elisa asked Jeff about his experience as a play therapist, and he described several positions he had held since earning an MSW—one in a psychiatric hospital, one in a private psychiatrist's office, and one in the guidance department of an elite private high school in the community. He spoke in such an intense, animated way that it was half an hour into the interview before Elisa noticed his earring and started to think more consciously about a feeling that had been building throughout the interview. *Oh. I wonder if he might be gay. I wonder if he's very open about it—that could be a problem around here.* Then she made herself pay attention to what Jeff was saying.

"But I am interested in working with kids on their own territory, and with kids who don't already have so many resources. I guess I'm just looking for a greater challenge, where I can make more of a difference."

Over the next hour, Jeff and Elisa discussed his qualifications, possible job duties, and salary range. Elisa was feeling better and better about the possibility of Jeff's being hired the longer they talked, and she sensed that Jeff was quite interested in the position.

Elisa was about ready to wrap up the interview when Jeff said, "I need to tell you about my last job." He paused a moment, then continued. "I worked at Lutheran Family Services for about 6 months, in a program developer position. And I was asked to resign."

Elisa swallowed, hoping what he was about to tell her wouldn't rule him out of consideration for the position.

"There was a teenage kid who came to the after-school program that I took an interest in. He was really awkward, and kinda smelly, and he seemed really lonely. It wasn't really my job to work individually with kids there, but after my day ended I would hang around and shoot some baskets with him, check his homework, stuff like that, and sometimes we'd sit out on the steps of the center and just talk. It was no great therapy or anything, but he started opening up a little, telling me about stuff that was going on at school and at home, and he would try some of the things I suggested, and he just seemed to be doing better—brighter, somehow. Then the director there told me he wanted me to stop seeing Anthony, that he thought it didn't look right giving him one-on-one attention like that, and some of the other kids were talking about it. I told him that I felt like it was making a difference for Anthony, and that I would just check with him and see if it would be okay with his mom if we came over to their house to talk instead of hanging around the center. He didn't like that either, said he didn't want me to work individually with any of the kids. I told him I wouldn't do it at the center anymore, but that I thought it was important to continue to support Anthony. And he said I would need to resign if I was going to defy him like that."

"So, I resigned." Jeff took a deep breath, and then went on. "I felt like he was implying something that he wouldn't say openly, and that it could get ugly, so it was better to go on and leave. Besides, I wasn't really happy not working with kids, anyway. Elisa, I didn't do anything wrong, not at all, but I won't get a good reference from LFS. I just wanted you to know."

"Thanks for telling me about this, Jeff," Elisa responded. "I still have to call all of your references, and I'll just have to see how that goes. Right now, based on what you're telling me, I respect your choice, and it isn't a problem for me. But I can't speak for anyone else, you understand, and I don't get to make the final decision."

"I understand. I hope that it can work out, because this job sounds like it would be a great fit for me. But whatever happens, thanks for the interview. I've enjoyed talking with you."

As Jeff shook Elisa's hand and then walked down the hall on his way out, Elisa realized that she'd been feeling that her earlier prayer had been answered, but that there were going to be some significant hurdles to get past. In Elisa's opinion, Jeff was perfect for the job, but the rest of his references would have to be stellar. And there was the fact that she suspected Jeff might be gay. His earring was the least-subtle clue—mostly she just had a feeling about it—but she felt it would probably stand out like a sore thumb to Charles. *So,* she wondered, *should I prepare him for the earring, or just hope maybe he doesn't notice it, or that it's not important to him in the overall scheme of things?*

Sure enough, when Elisa called Jeff's references the following Monday, they were glowing. She called his practicum supervisor, his previous employers (except for Lutheran Family Services), and a colleague at Lutheran Family Services (given as a personal reference). They were all very positive about Jeff, mentioning his maturity, sensitivity, rapport with kids, creativity, and willingness to work hard and to go above and beyond what was required, as well as his passion for social justice and for doing what was right. One of the references told Elisa, "Jeff is just pure gold!" Elisa was happy that her impressions of Jeff were confirmed, but she was still anxious about Charles's impending response.

CHARLES'S DECISION

After mulling it over during the weekend, Elisa decided not to call the earring to Charles's attention. She scheduled Jeff's interview with Charles for Thursday morning, expecting to hear Charles's decision about Jeff by mid-afternoon. But one week later, on Friday afternoon, Elisa still had not received any word from Charles about the hire. Finally, she decided to call Charles and ask his decision. But before she had the chance, Helen Jaynes, Charles's secretary, called to say that he was on his way up to her office.

When he arrived in Elisa's office, Charles surprised her by shutting the door and sitting down. The office was eerily quiet for what seemed like a long time, and then Charles started, "Elisa, I'm afraid that we won't be able to hire Jeff. He just isn't right for the position."

"What?!" Elisa exclaimed, then caught herself. "Jeff's the best person we found. I think he's exactly the right person for the job. You don't agree?"

"Well, it's just that, well. . . ." Charles paused, and then continued calmly, "We are not going to start a fashion trend at this agency. Jeff's earring is completely inappropriate and unacceptable."

"What does his earring have to do with his ability to perform his job duties?" Elisa blurted out. She was not surprised that Charles would think that, but still dumbfounded that he would actually say it out loud. "Charles, he is hands down the best person for the job." At that point, Elisa could tell Charles was becoming angry, yet she pressed on. "It's just not fair to let something like an earring stand in the way—not fair to him, and not good for us either. That's discrimination."

"There is no law about discriminating against people who wear earrings," he said forcefully. As Charles responded, his face reddened and his voice grew louder.

"Charles," Elisa insisted once again, "he is the best person for this position. I interviewed six other people and no one else even comes close to him. I checked his references and they were very strong. I know our kids will love him—he's so gentle, fun, and kind. He's the right person for this job. I'm sure of it. After meeting him, I can't imagine hiring any of the others I interviewed. Any of them would be a far-second choice at best."

But even as she protested, Elisa could tell that Charles was not going to budge. "I don't care how qualified he is," Charles snapped, his eyes flashing, and the veins in his forehead standing out, "I'm not hiring a man who wears an earring to represent this agency!" And he stood up to leave.

Elisa sat there staring at Charles in disbelief. As Charles reached for the door handle he turned to Elisa, and shouted, "If you don't find someone else, then I will!" Charles then stormed out of the office, leaving Elisa in stunned silence. Watching him leave, Elisa realized that her instincts had been right— this was about way more than just an earring.

THE DILEMMA

Elisa drove home that day in tears, feeling some anger about the injustice of Charles's response, and unsure of how to handle the situation. She felt obligated to call Jeff, and inform him about the situation. She explained to Jeff that Charles was having a problem with Jeff's "earring."

Jeff chuckled at that, saying, "I've heard that 'concern' before. My little earring is a big problem for anyone who has a problem with someone who's gay."

"I'm so sorry, Jeff." As she continued, Elisa's voice trembled. "It's so unfair and so wrong. Your references were great, and I think you'd be a real asset to us. I just am not at all sure I can bring him around. He was really angry this afternoon. He may fire me in addition to not hiring you."

She sensed Jeff was trying to be calm and not react to her with a lot of emotion, that he understood she wanted him and had really pushed Charles to hire him, but she also thought she could hear the hurt in his voice as they made an agreement to talk the next afternoon.

As Elisa hung up the phone, thoughts flooded her mind. *What am I going to do? Charles's decision is discriminatory and wrong . . . but is it worth sacrificing my job to fight his decision? And if I lose my job what will I do financially? But, if I keep my job how will I be able to live with myself? If Charles knew about me, he'd probably let me go, too, so am I being unfair just to keep quiet and invisible, instead of taking a stand like Jeff has done?*

Case 12

Revealing Problems (A)[1]

CARL D. MAAS
TERRY A. WOLFER

In February 2000, after 5 months in therapy, 17-year-old Roberta Hyde stunned therapist Samantha Schield by matter-of-factly recounting how she had found pornographic images on her family's computer.

"Of all these pictures of naked people, I guess what bothered me most were the ones of children, specifically boys," Roberta concluded her revelation.

After sitting there a moment, trying to absorb the information, Samantha probed gently, "What did you do?"

Roberta shrugged, "I didn't know what to do. I just looked at them and didn't know what to do." Then, looking directly at Samantha, she added, "I'm telling you because I don't *know* what to do."

SAMANTHA SCHIELD

Raised by parents who both worked in social services for the state of West Virginia, Samantha Schield had developed a passion for advocacy at an early age. Her interest in mental health issues and the stigma attached to persons

1. Development of this decision case was supported in part by funding from the University of South Carolina College of Social Work. It was prepared solely to provide material for class discussion and not to suggest either effective or ineffective handling of the situation depicted. While based on field research regarding an actual situation, names and certain facts may have been disguised to protect confidentiality. The authors and editors wish to thank the anonymous case reporter for her cooperation in making this account available for the benefit of social work students and instructors. Copyright © 2005 Thomson Learning.

with mental illness led her to work in the mental health field. After obtaining her BA degree in psychology, Samantha worked for 5 years at River Run, a private, nonprofit psychiatric rehabilitation center in Morgantown, West Virginia. River Run helped people with severe and persistent mental illnesses live as independently as possible within the community. Samantha began in direct casework, but was quickly promoted to administrative positions. At times though, she felt unprepared for administration, and that concerned her. It seemed a common assumption that clinicians would just pick up supervisory and administration skills. Samantha's experiences with some of her own supervisors indicated otherwise. Far too often, she had seen great therapists promoted to administrative positions who had become, in her opinion, awful supervisors. She knew supervisors who treated their employees like clients and lacked the skills necessary for administration. After four promotions and growing frustration with state mental health services, Samantha decided to pursue a master's degree from the West Virginia University School of Social Work. Samantha believed that an MSW would provide her greater opportunity to address the systemic problems her clients faced on a day-to-day basis.

As a result of her work experience, Samantha knew from the beginning that she wanted to focus her MSW experience on administration. At the same time, she felt an obligation to acquire solid clinical experience as a first-year MSW intern. In particular, she was intrigued by a new therapeutic approach to treating the very clients she had felt most frustrated by at the rehab center. This new therapy was called dialectical behavior therapy (DBT). On hearing of it, Samantha decided to pursue a field placement at Kanawha County Community Mental Health Center (KCCMHC), a public agency that locally pioneered use of DBT with people having multi-diagnostic needs.

In addition to the usual community mental health population, KCCMHC specialized in the very types of clients that many physicians and clinicians shuddered to treat. Samantha hated it when she heard other therapists describe such clients as "manipulative." Samantha had often responded, "Manipulative implies being artful. These individuals are not artful. If anything, we therapists are manipulative. We have the skills to be effective. They do not have these skills yet." Nevertheless, when she thought about these clients, Samantha often asked herself, *What is it that I am missing? What is it that I am not doing to engage this client? Why aren't they getting it? They take up so much of my time and I don't see that much of a change in their behaviors.* Samantha was excited about finding a way to help individuals who seemed to have experienced a lifetime of pain.

As Samantha told a colleague, "DBT is all about participating in the moment, synthesizing opposites. DBT helps people who think in extremes, allowing them to achieve more balanced thinking. Because of its structure, DBT is very different from many forms of psychotherapy."

"But," Samantha acknowledged, "DBT is not for everyone. It's been tested primarily in a female population. Adolescents have used this intervention well. DBT is being tested now in individuals diagnosed with dissociative disorder and antisocial behavior. Though it's been tested and has some empirical evidence of success—making it very popular with insurance companies—it's still not for everyone" (for more information about DBT, see Samantha's class paper in Appendix A).

Most of the clients that Samantha worked with at KCCMHC had a Cluster B personality disorder and an Axis I diagnosis, such as depression or bipolar disorder. With all of her clients, the Axis I diagnosis interfered with daily living, causing many therapists to dismiss these types of clients as manipulative and unwilling to address therapeutic issues. Samantha was surprised at how well this theoretical approach appeared to work with these types of clients. She learned a lot and thoroughly enjoyed the 9-month internship at KCCMHC. Subsequently, during the second year of her MSW program, Samantha decided to run Stage II groups for DBT clients at KCCMHC as a volunteer.

After graduation in May 1999, Samantha obtained a full-time position in social work administration for a statewide advocacy organization. She enjoyed the work but she remained committed to DBT and interested in working with individuals who could benefit from that treatment approach. As a result, Samantha responded to an offer made by Dorothy Turner to work part time for the Behavioral Health Clinic (BHC) of West Virginia. Turner had been Samantha's preceptor at the KCCMHC internship and was co-owner of BHC.

THE BEHAVIORAL HEALTH CLINIC
OF WEST VIRGINIA

Founded in 1994, BHC was designed to treat individuals who would benefit from dialectical behavior therapy. Due to the success of the program, the small for-profit practice quickly expanded from its base in Charleston into a clinic that served individuals across the state. The clinic primarily used contract counselors who worked evenings and weekends. The clinic provided services to a wide range of clients, but mostly served clients with health insurance or means to pay for the services.

BHC included four full-time therapists and four part-time therapists, with Samantha among the latter. Of the eight therapists, four had MSWs, two had PhDs in psychology, one a degree in psychiatry, and one a master's in counseling. Dorothy, the center's founder and co-owner, had trained them all in DBT. Dorothy used the staff's mixed professional background to the center's advantage, as each therapist provided a plethora of ideas during case and staff consultations. BHC used a team counselor approach that required all the counselors to meet together either between sessions or at weekly case meetings to conduct team consultations. These consultations were structured to reflect the peer review approach that enhanced both the quality of service and harnessed the depth of knowledge that the counselors had as a team. In addition, the co-owners of the clinic had many years of experience with DBT therapy and led the team consultations.

Consistent with DBT philosophy, the clinic's co-owners required that therapists attend team consultations, usually on a weekly basis, and seek consultation regarding their own cases on an "as needed" basis. Also, each therapist met with either Dorothy or Robin Neeley, the other co-owner, for individual consultation sessions. These sessions tended to be more informal, either occurring during a weekly scheduled individual session or when convenient for the people involved. The purpose of consultation was twofold, providing both skills training and feedback to each therapist for individual client interventions.

A highly structured intervention, DBT attempted to address the poor emotional feedback that caused "dysregulation" of clients' lives. The treatment was also intensive, requiring clients to attend group and individual sessions while completing three stages of therapy: Level 1 consisted of skills learning, Level 2 focused on self-awareness and monitoring of destructive urges related to past traumas, and Level 3 focused on generalization of skill sets to personal life. Since working with BHC as an intern and volunteer, Samantha now felt very comfortable working as a contract therapist. She enjoyed the long-term contact with the agency.

After passing her licensing exam in July 1999, Samantha worked nights, running two groups and providing individual therapy to nine clients per week. Having previously worked with the adult population, Samantha now found that she had a knack for working with adolescents and their families. She constantly felt challenged by the clinical work and felt she was learning new things every week.

Samantha's work at BHC also helped her acquire clinical experience for LISW licensure, one of her professional goals. Dr. Mills, her LISW supervisor, was not a member of the BHC team, which helped her to objectively reflect on her clinical work. Therefore, Samantha was able to both pursue a professional goal and continue working with this fascinating population.

ROBERTA HYDE

In September 1999, while working as a contract therapist for BHC, Samantha met Roberta Hyde, a 17-year-old white girl. In the previous 2 years, Roberta had been hospitalized twice to stabilize major depressive episodes. The first hospitalization occurred following the death of Roberta's maternal grandmother, Mrs. Granby. As Samantha recalled, "She had assumed a huge responsibility in taking care of her grandmother. Her grandmother was an important figure in Roberta's life." Roberta expressed anger about her grandmother's death and also some resentment regarding the heavy responsibility she had assumed for her grandmother's care.

Although her parents were not immediately aware of this, soon after Mrs. Granby passed away Roberta began "cutting." Roberta cut herself on her arms and legs, each cut between 1 and 2 inches in length, while alone in her room. Typically, these were not deep gouges, but more like scratches. In addition, Roberta had also been caught stealing from a store and, at the time of referral, was performing community service to expunge the misdemeanor from her record.

When her parents found out about her cutting, following a shoplifting incident, they decided to hospitalize her a second time. The treating psychiatrist told the family that Roberta had characteristics of borderline personality disorder (BPD). He advised the family that DBT had a successful track record of treating parasuicidal behaviors—any type of self-harm that causes tissue damage—and other behaviors associated with BPD. On release from the local psychiatric hospital, her family sought DBT services for Roberta at BHC.

Samantha remembered, "When Roberta first came to the clinic she was very withdrawn, she did not like to talk a lot. Roberta tended to change her hair color a lot. She was overall very reserved, but she was super intelligent and very articulate." Samantha remembered thinking, *She is not happy that she is cutting and 'lifting. She says she wants to stop. She seems to really want to change these behaviors.* During the initial assessment, Samantha routinely asked questions about sexual trauma. Like some 40 percent of cutters, Roberta denied experiencing any sexual abuse as a child.

Roberta took medications to manage her depression. She did not seem to suffer any adverse side effects and was compliant in taking her prescribed medications. However, Samantha soon learned that Roberta took other things along with her medications—she smoked pot, drank, and stole or bought other people's prescription drugs, specifically her father's Adivan. This information did not surprise Samantha. This was a common trend—abusing prescription drugs. Other clients often told her, "It's a cheap way to get high—to feel better."

THE FIRST SESSION

"During the first session," Samantha recalled, "all of the family members were present. We spoke about DBT and social work responsibilities, mandated reporting, and my other responsibilities as a therapist. We also discussed when the family wanted to come into the sessions. We discussed whether they wanted to come in for 15 minutes of every 60-minute session. Eventually, we planned for Roberta to see me for 2 weeks and then have a check-in session with the other family members."

Samantha remembered that when the family arrived, Roberta's father took the seat that Samantha normally used. "This was funny, since I was nervous to begin with, because I knew Roberta's father was a licensed social worker.

I asked them to seat themselves where they wanted to sit, and he did! He sat where I was supposed to sit!"

Samantha sat in another seat.

The father spoke first, and he led most of the discussions when Samantha asked questions of other family members. Samantha felt uncomfortable when Mr. Hyde would state, "Perhaps we should discuss this first" and then continue in a direction that was perfectly logical, but not necessarily the direction Samantha wanted to go at that point. Samantha kept telling herself, *Start where the client is. Don't let your ego get in the way of being effective.* Samantha recalled, "Roberta's father tended to speak a lot. Even though he was very validating of Roberta, he seemed to be preachy and this turned me off somewhat. I kept struggling with why I had these judgments about him. I was challenged to get the mother and the daughter to speak up in the session. I imagined that this scenario seemed to be representative of what it was like at their home."

As Samantha subsequently recorded in the chart record, "The Hydes are a typical middle-class family. The parents met in college. They got married and had children. Their marriage overall has been fulfilling, though with some rough spots. Mrs. Hyde works as a bookkeeper at a local church ever since Harry, the oldest child, finished high school. Mr. Hyde works as a mid-level administrator in a residential treatment center for children. The family regularly eats dinner together and shares a variety of family activities."

After Roberta's second hospitalization, the family reported having had an open dialogue about the various problems that Mr. Hyde had experienced as well as what Roberta was going through. Mr. Hyde had a history of depression. As an adolescent, he became addicted to codeine and had his first major depressive episode.

After graduating with a degree in theology, Mr. Hyde began working in social services. Because he did not have a degree in social work, counseling, or psychology, Mr. Hyde became licensed as a social worker under a "grandfather" clause in the state legislation. He worked as a clinician with troubled children at Charleston Home for Children (CHC), a residential treatment center, for more than 10 years before being promoted into administration with the same organization. Mr. Hyde took a special interest in Roberta's therapy and encouraged her to do DBT. In Stage I, DBT clients often see their therapists twice a week, once for group and once for individual sessions. Demonstrating his commitment to Roberta's therapy, Mr. Hyde ensured Roberta never missed an appointment.

It was obvious to Samantha from the very beginning that Roberta adored her father. Roberta often opened sessions by reporting their conversations about her DBT skills and homework assignments.

In contrast, Roberta's relationship with her mother was less intense and less positive, not what Roberta wanted it to be. Roberta told Samantha that she wanted a deeper relationship with her mother. With that in mind, Roberta and Samantha worked on a list of questions that Roberta could use for talking with her mother. In particular, Roberta never felt like she could ask her mom questions about being a teenager.

Roberta saw her mother as being perfect and never doing anything wrong. As Roberta confided in one session, "My mom rarely discusses things with me. I don't have any problem telling her about my life but she never asks me anything. And she never tells me anything about her own life. It's like she doesn't want to share with me her experiences or go into any depth about mine. She is such a goodie-goodie. She never talks about the shoplifting or cutting. Sometimes I just wish we could just discuss this stuff."

Furthermore, Mrs. Hyde never acknowledged what Roberta was doing. Roberta assumed that this meant that her mother judged her, and Roberta wanted to be validated by her mother. One of Roberta's goals was to be more involved with her mother and for them to have a closer relationship.

Interestingly, Mrs. Hyde was the parent who usually brought Roberta to therapy sessions. Samantha wondered whether Mrs. Hyde felt guilty about having Roberta provide so much care for her mother, Mrs. Granby.

Roberta had mixed feelings toward Harry, her 20-year-old brother. He had graduated from high school but held a job only sporadically. When he did have a job, it was usually at night. According to Roberta, Harry had no responsibilities around the house and tended to spend all of his time in his room. There, he mostly wrote. With apparent pride, Roberta told Samantha on several occasions, "He's a fantastic writer! You should read his work. I just know he will be published some day. He's the next Stephen King." On the other hand, Roberta also expressed dissatisfaction with their sibling relationship. As one of her therapeutic goals, Roberta wanted to work on her relationship with Harry.

Samantha would respond, "If someone else is part of your goal, they have to be involved in the goal setting and the sessions."

But Harry would never commit to attending sessions and this bothered Roberta a great deal. Roberta would say, "What does he do up there all day? I mean, mom and dad make me come here and he doesn't even have a life, except for writing. I am so worried about him. All he does is stay holed up in that room . . . on the computer. I see how much I am learning and *he* needs DBT. I get pissed off when I think about how different the expectations are for me versus him. It makes me sad. You know, he used to cut, too, but he doesn't any more."

CONSULTING AFTER THE FIRST SESSION

Samantha discussed the first family session with the clinic staff because she felt concerned about her reaction to the social worker/father and his relatively long professional experience. Samantha told her colleagues, "The father was at first, very intimidating. He was an experienced social worker with 30 years experience. He studied theology and was 'grandfathered' into the professional license when the state established the new regulations for licensure. Still, who was I? I had just graduated and he was a big dog where he worked."

"Dorothy reminded me that, 'it's normal to feel green, like you don't have enough experience.' Another therapist pointed out that I needed to practice being 'nonjudgmental, which included not judging oneself.' This reminded me of a basic tenant of DBT, which states that, 'when you're emotional, it's hard to be wise'."

Samantha remembered that, "Roberta had a high opinion of her father. Via the response cards (cards used to track urges to carry out a non-desirable behavior during each week of therapy), I was impressed at how important Roberta's dad was in her life. Her dad did a lot to help Roberta talk to her mother. Roberta constantly opened her sessions with me by recounting what Roberta and her father discussed and how he helped her with therapeutic homework that I assigned."

"She rarely got put on restriction. One week, Roberta came into the session and I noticed that on her diary card she had stolen pills one day and then each day after that she had high urges to use but indicated that she had not used. Roberta had taken 10 pills from her dad. She had them for 5 days and Roberta was upset because her dad hadn't confronted her about taking them. We did a chain analysis and she decided to return them to him, instead of using or selling them. It took her 2 days, but she returned them and told her father she took them and asked him why he did not confront her. Roberta told me that he said it was because he knew she would do the right thing and that he would not always be around to censor her behaviors. He was very understanding and validated her use of skills.

"Overall Roberta was very fond of him. She felt that he would listen to her, and not judge her like her mother. Roberta would have consequences, but she was heard out and understood most by her father," Samantha remarked.

THERAPEUTIC GOALS

At the second session, following DBT structure, Samantha continued working to build rapport with Roberta. She also began working explicitly to establish Roberta's goals. To do so, Samantha used some standard DBT questions: "What do you want to work on? What do you see as big problems in your life? What's interfering with being effective? Roberta began working to control her urges to cut herself, steal things, and to use illicit drugs. These became goals in a goal sheet or a set of therapeutic goals developed by the client and used as a guide to determining therapeutic outcomes and success. They talked about what Roberta wanted to be when she grew up and what she wanted to study in college. Samantha introduced several routine DBT assignments that helped Roberta look at her behaviors in relation to her emotional state.

"I have messed up some relationships due to my stealing" wrote Roberta on her first goal sheet. "I have taken things, like lipstick, eyeliner, and other small things from friends when I would visit them at their homes."

Some of these relationships she wished to repair and others she did not. Samantha was concerned about some of the relationships that Roberta wanted to repair. In particular, Roberta wanted to repair a relationship with a young woman who exhibited the same parasuicidal behavior. This concerned Samantha, because a domino effect often occurred when individuals with parasuicidal urges started to discuss their pain and urge to cut. Providing an example, Samantha explained, "In group skills training this is often a concern, where one client's past trauma gets transferred to another client. The second client may not be equipped yet to handle this detailed retelling of a past trauma and it can trigger their own painful memories. It makes it difficult for the client to tolerate the extreme pain that is relived, especially if they haven't learned skills in this particular area."

"Ultimately this relationship between Roberta and her friend proved to be a learning experience for both Roberta and me," Samantha said. "I learned to give more credit to Roberta, as she became a role model for her friend. Roberta also learned that this friend was not someone that she needed in her life, since she was not able to support Roberta when Roberta had needs. Ultimately the friendship drained Roberta and Roberta let the relationship go."

Repairing relationships provided a focus for work in the DBT skills learning group. Roberta worked on a goal while learning new coping skills. The process included the daily note cards that allow the consumer and the therapist to do a "chain analysis." Basically, a chain analysis involved identifying the urges that resulted in an action. Samantha noted, "Often these chain analyses are very unemotional. The chain analysis gathers information in a nonjudgmental way for a consumer to gather insight to their urges and behavior. It allows consumers to see patterns and sequences in behavior to auto-intervene urges and actions." Once urges and consequences are analyzed, therapists help clients identify and learn ways to change the pattern of behaviors that led to acting on the urge.

Although Roberta wanted to change, the initial progress was slow. To Samantha, it appeared that Roberta's goals in therapy conflicted with her self-construct: "I suspect that it added to her individuality and being seen as different and unique at school, being a cutter and stealing stuff." More specifically, as Samantha understood it, "there were two conflicts. First, for teenagers, there is a value to being different. The second one, I think, was a historical conflict, revolving around an admiration of the children that her dad worked with through the residential treatment center."

Roberta told Samantha, "Growing up, both of my parents worked at the treatment center and would often bring those children home with them for respite or to partake in a family activity." Roberta went on, "I think that

I admired those children in that they had suffered something and that they needed a special amount of attention." Roberta was aware that, "Those children gained a lot of my father's attention."

The overwhelming correlation between parasuicidal behaviors and sexual trauma also made Samantha wonder if Roberta had been abused as a child. At times, Samantha had wondered if any children from the treatment center might have abused Roberta as a little girl. She also wondered whether any of the immediate family members might have sexually abused Roberta.

Nevertheless, Samantha had not explored these possibilities with Roberta. As she explained, "In DBT, therapists do not explore past traumas until clients have acquired the skills necessary to do trauma work. Stage I DBT, usually the first 6 to 12 months, focuses on skills acquisition. Most of these clients have experienced traumatic past experiences that increase their urges significantly. If a client has not practiced or learned the skills taught in Stage I, these often life-threatening behaviors will increase. That is why it's important for DBT therapists to follow the empirically proven structure. Deviation from this structure could result in a client committing suicide—a result from a parasuicidal act."

"Research indicates a correlation between childhood sexual abuse and cutting, but not all cutters have been sexually abused." Samantha always had a problem with clinicians who, assuming that abuse had occurred, would ask stereotypical questions in team consultations such as, "Who was the abuser?" Samantha felt strongly about not leading clients in a direction or making assumptions about someone being a "perpetrator" within the family. Often, when abuse had occurred, it involved a distant relative, like an uncle, or a neighbor.

Roberta had worked with Samantha to develop a comprehensive list of goals, including increasing her ability to tolerate stressful situations, thus controlling urges to cut and to steal; improving her interpersonal skills by learning how to attend to, maintain, and repair existing relationships; and improving her ability to regulate her emotions, through identifying purpose and effectiveness of emotion in the moment. Samantha and Roberta revisited these goals every 4 weeks and assessed Roberta's progress toward her goals by self-report and a trend study with the diary cards.

THE REVELATION

By February 21, 2000, Samantha perceived that Roberta had made impressive progress. Roberta had only cut herself twice since starting therapy. She was building a better relationship with her mother. She still was struggling to stop stealing, but making progress. More important, as Samantha observed, "Roberta had started to create a new self-construct. She let go of her identity of being a 'cutter'."

Roberta came to session that night with her diary card in hand as usual. Samantha reviewed it and saw no reason to do a chain analysis. Roberta had not acted on any urges and, even better, she had not rated anything above a 1.

After the usual opening pleasantries, Samantha asked, "Would you like to discuss a situation this week in which you used a skill?"

Roberta replied, "Well, something interesting happened."

"Like what?" Samantha probed gently.

"I am not sure if I want to talk about it."

Because this hesitation seemed out of character, Samantha reminded Roberta, "Remember, everything we discuss in session is confidential, unless it involves something that could be or is harmful to others or to you."

"Well, I was on my computer at home. . . ."

"And?" Samantha prompted.

"Well, this is not the first time that this has happened," Roberta continued slowly.

"What happened?"

"I was on our computer at home, when I saw some clips of pornography."

"What do you mean 'pornography'?"

"Of naked people."

"What kinds of naked people?"

"All kinds of naked people," Roberta paused. "Of all these pictures of naked people, I guess what bothered me most were the ones of children, specifically boys. They were naked. They were. . . . They were doing stuff, sexual acts."

"What are 'sexual acts'?"

"Sexual stuff."

"Who was doing the 'sexual stuff'?"

"The boys and the other people."

Samantha felt stunned. It appeared to Samantha that Roberta had found this difficult to disclose. Roberta looked embarrassed and, as she spoke, seemed more and more timid.

After a moment's hesitation, Samantha continued, "Did you see these clips while online?"

"No, I was going to copy some music from a CD, when the clips came up in the Windows Media player. They were stored, you know, in the cache. They were like left over after someone is online and didn't erase the cache or the file."

"Oh," Samantha replied. "Who do you think put it there?"

"Well, I think that they're my father's," Roberta replied.

Samantha sat back and thought to herself, "*Holy shit! What do I do with this*"?

As Samantha tried to collect her thoughts, she thought, "*What the hell am I going to do? Her father is a licensed social worker for goodness sake. He works in a residential treatment facility for children and he is downloading pornography? And some of it involves children?*"

Samantha looked to Roberta. As Roberta toyed with her bracelet, Samantha reassured herself, "*Silence is sometimes very good in therapy. I don't want to invalidate her. She is obviously feeling scared.*"

Then out loud she said, "I can see why you're upset. This is a very complicated situation. Let me think about this for a minute."

Trying to absorb the information, Samantha wondered, "*What do I do now? Do I get more information? Do I review her concerns about the issues?*" While feeling the burden of having this information Samantha realized, "*Roberta has trusted me with it.*"

Finally, Samantha asked, "What did you do?"

Roberta shrugged, "I didn't know what to do. I just looked at them and didn't know what to do. Well, actually, I did what I had done the other times I found them. I deleted the clips."

Samantha probed, "Are you sure that they were your father's? Are you sure that they are not your brother's?"

"Oh, yeah. My brother was there when I saw them, and he got pissed. He was grossed out, and couldn't believe that it was on the computer."

"Have either of you talked to your mom or dad about what you found?" Samantha asked.

"No," Roberta said, "we haven't talked to anyone else. But Harry suggested I talk to you." Looking directly at Samantha, Roberta added, "I'm telling you because I don't *know* what to do."

Appendix A

Introduction to Dialectical
Behavioral Therapy[2]
By Samantha Schield

Dialectical Behavior Therapy (DBT) is a broad-based cognitive behavior therapy with an eastern flavor. Developed by Marsha Linehan, DBT is an empirically based approach for treating Borderline Personality Disorder. DBT's approach is also based on the biosocial theory of personality functioning: that a person with a biological predisposition to emotional sensitivity is invalidated over a period of time, resulting in Borderline Personality Disorder. Using four modes of treatment, DBT targets five main areas of "dysregulation."

MODES OF TREATMENT

DBT is a manualized treatment program that requires a one-year commitment on the part of clients, as well as therapists. DBT includes: (1) a weekly, two-hour "skills training group"; (2) a weekly, one-hour individual therapy session with a DBT therapist; (3) team consultation/supervision meetings for therapists; and (4) telephone consultation as needed between the client and individual therapist (Shearin & Linehan, 1994; KCCMHC, 1997). The commitment to DBT from the client involves an agreement to not only contract for one year, but to work on reducing parasuicidal (self-injurious acts) behaviors and to work on behaviors that are identified as "therapy interfering" during the course of the treatment (Kiehn & Swales, 1995). This makes DBT unique.

Skills Training Group

It is necessary to briefly describe the sequence and purpose of skills training and why it is important to the interventions employed by DBT therapists. Skills training sessions include a broad range of skills acquisition, specifically in the skill areas of mindfulness, interpersonal effectiveness, emotion regulation, and distress tolerance. Each skill area is considered a module in group therapy and lasts eight weeks in duration.

Derived from Buddhist meditation, core mindfulness skills are always taught first because they serve as the foundation upon which other skills are built. Core mindfulness skills are psychological techniques, which focus on allowing the individual to take control of their thoughts by acquiring, strengthening, and then generalizing the skills (Linehan, 1993). For example, the skill, OBSERVE, requires noticing the experience without getting caught up in the experience—to experience without reacting to the experience (Linehan, 1993). The main objective is to notice each feeling, thought, and behavior and watch it rise and fall like a wave (Linehan, 1993). This is extremely important for individuals diagnosed with

---

2. This is a slightly edited version of an actual paper Samantha wrote for an MSW practice class.

Dissociative Identity Disorder (DID) because of their high levels of dissociation. These skills enable the client "to become more clearly aware of experience and to develop the ability to stay with that experience in the present moment" (Kiehn and Swales, 1995, p. 6). The overarching goal is to participate in life with full awareness. These skills tell us how to go about controlling the attention process (Linehan, 1993). Another skill, ONE-MINDFULLY, focuses on doing one thing at a time with awareness (Linehan, 1993). Mindfulness determines upon what the attention will be focused and detects when attention strays (Linehan, 1993).

Interpersonal Effectiveness skills teach one how to do what works in order to get one's needs met, while maintaining both parties' self-respect (Linehan, 1993). Learning how to say, "No" is also taught. The core concept in this module is about interacting and communicating effectively with others (Linehan, 1993). This module is similar to other types of assertiveness training.

The Emotion Regulation module focuses on being able to identify, experience, and regulate emotions in the moment (Linehan, 1993). An example of this would be identifying an emotion, thought, or urge, then being aware of it in the moment, and making a conscious decision to act opposite to that impulse, urge, emotion, thought, or condition (Linehan, 1993). Clients learn about the birth of an emotion, what primary emotions are, the functions of emotions, and then skills to help reduce intense emotions that are not useful. These skills are essential in reducing escalation of emotions attributed to flashbacks and insight gained from remembering traumatic abuse experienced during childhood (Linehan, 1993). If an individual is triggered, they are equipped to use these skills to regulate their changing emotions.

The fourth and final module, Distress Tolerance, focuses on two main themes: acceptance and change. The first is the most important. If one is not at a place where he or she can regulate emotion, he or she must tolerate the stress and survive the crisis (Linehan, 1994). One must first accept the circumstances as they are before change can be problem solved. In-depth descriptions of these modules and skills can be found in the Skill's Training Manual (Linehan, 1993).

Individual Psychotherapy

The primary therapist must be a DBT therapist who is involved in the treatment team consultation and program (Linehan, 1993). Individual therapy is the main artery of the treatment program in that the bulk of the "hard" work is done there (Kiehn & Swales, 1995). DBT therapists must have a thorough understanding and practice of behavioral therapy and a variety of other treatment approaches and theoretical constructs. The relationship between the therapist and the client is some times the only variable in contingency management strategies during treatment. Therefore, it is essential to the effectiveness of the program.

Team Consultation

Team consultation provides "therapy for the therapists." Consultation serves as a system of checks and balances for both the therapist and the client and reduces therapist "burn out." Together, the team critically reviews their cases to see what is effective and what is not. Therapists reflect on their cases in light of DBT fundamentals (Linehan, 1993). Special attention is paid to pejorative or punitive experiences a client may have perceived from a therapist and behavioral/chain analyses evaluate reinforcers and punishers—pinpointing the antecedents/common links to a specific behavior (Linehan, 1994).

Phone Consultation

Between therapy sessions, clients are allowed to contact their therapist for one of two basic reasons: (1) to attend to the relationship to reduce rumination and (2) to receive coaching on a particular skill. It is up to the therapist to observe and set limits/boundaries regarding phone consultation (KCCMHC, 1997). Phone consultation can be used in contingency management strategies, as well.

Stages of Therapy

There are essentially three stages of treatment during the DBT program (Kiehn & Swales, 1995). The first stage is the assessment, orientation, and understanding of the commitment made to the therapy. Stage I focuses on acquiring the skills necessary to deal with process issues. For example, a concentrated effort will be placed on reducing behaviors that are suicidal, therapy interfering, and quality of life interfering (Kiehn & Swales, 1995). Stage I typically lasts six months to one year, after which clients are equipped with the skills to enter Stage II (Linehan, 1993).

Stage II therapy deals with posttraumatic stress-related issues (Kiehn & Swales, 1995). Clients must have mastered Stage I before moving to this stage (Linehan, 1993). This allows them the ability to begin to process horrific childhood memories, memories of dissociating, flashbacks, and alters. With their new skills, clients can be helped to deal with these memories through exposure (Kiehn & Swales, 1995).

In Stage III, therapy focuses on issues of self-esteem, maintenance, and individual treatment goals (Kiehn & Swales, 1995). The overarching goal of each stage is to increase dialectical thinking and identification of self.

REFERENCES

Kanawha County Community Mental Health Center. (1997). Understanding Dialectical Behavior Therapy [brochure]. Charleston, WV: Author.

Kiehn, B., & Swales, M. (1995). The use of a multi-stage confrontation technique in the context of an adolescent unit. *Journal of Adolescence, 18*(3), 317–327.

Linehan, M. M. (1993). *Skills training manual for treating borderline personality disorder.* New York: Guilford Press.

Linehan, M. M. (1994). *Cognitive-behavioral treatment of borderline personality disorder.* New York: Guilford Press.

Shearin, E. N., & Linehan, M. M. (1994). Dialectical behavior therapy for borderline personality disorder: Theoretical and empirical foundations. *Acta Psychiatrica Scandinavica, 89*(379, Supplement), 61–68.